LAWS TO LOVE BY:

THE

TEN

COMMANDMENTS

Phyllis Vos Wezeman
Judith Harris Chase

DEDICATION

To Quin David Sky Wezeman, my first grandchild ...

May you always be guided by God's "laws to love by."   P.V.W.

To Mary Jane Harris, my mother...

who taught me about the Ten Commandments by "living" them.   J.H.C.

LAWS TO LOVE BY: The Ten Commandments
by Judith Harris Chase and Phyllis Vos Wezeman

Copyright ©1996 Educational Ministries, Inc.

ISBN 1-57438-001-X

Educational Ministries, Inc.

165 Plaza Drive

Prescott, AZ 86303

800-221-0910

TABLE OF CONTENTS

OVERVIEW.. 5

Chapter One : INTRODUCTION TO THE TEN COMMANDMENTS............ 7

Chapter Two: THE FIRST COMMANDMENT................................15

Chapter Three: THE SECOND COMMANDMENT 21

Chapter Four: THE THIRD COMMANDMENT 27

Chapter Five: THE FOURTH COMMANDMENT 32

Chapter Six: THE FIFTH COMMANDMENT..............................38

Chapter Seven: THE SIXTH COMMANDMENT 45

Chapter Eight: THE SEVENTH COMMANDMENT 51

Chapter Nine: THE EIGHTH COMMANDMENT..........................58

Chapter Ten: THE NINTH COMMANDMENT..............................66

Chapter Eleven: THE TENTH COMMANDMENT 72

Chapter Twelve: SUMMARY OF THE LAW 79

Chapter Thirteen: TEN COMMANDMENT REVIEW 85

Chapter Fourteen: ENHANCEMENTS......................................92

RESOURCES 94

OVERVIEW

Although the Ten Commandments were given by God, through Moses, to the people of Israel in Old Testament times, these important words of Scripture have had an impact on every age throughout history and are still relevant today. Not only did they become the basis of all Hebrew Laws, they have been and continue to be the essence of all laws of civilization. Recorded in Exodus 20:1-17 and Deuteronomy 5:6-21 and summarized in Matthew 22:37-40, the Ten Commandments have been called by many names: decalogue, laws, guides, guidelines, rules, signposts, tablets, maps. They have been interpreted in numerous ways as well: negative, authoritarian, controlling, demanding, ordering. In Hebrew, however, the word "law" means "to teach." Thus, God gave the Ten Commandments to the Hebrew travelers, and to us, to teach people how to live, and more importantly, how to love. This Covenant between God and His people was given in love. God loved the descendants of Abraham, Isaac and Jacob so much that He provided them with a set of values that would become the basis of all human relationships. In return, God's people would show their love for God by keeping the Commandments, or living by these guidelines.

Laws To Love By: The Ten Commandments contains a series of activities based on each of God's guides for living. Participants explore and experience inviting, informing, inspiring projects that are used to impart information and ideas. Laws To Love By is intended to help participants explore the Ten Commandments in creative, concrete and challenging ways, and to experience them as values for living rather than as restrictive laws. Activities are designed to help learners look at the Commandments as liberating possibilities that enrich and enable human growth; liberating us for faith, holiness, gratitude, care, life, fidelity, honesty, truth, purity, generosity, and much more.

In this resource instruction takes place through involvement in a series of Learning Centers. A Learning Center may be defined as the focal point of activity for the purpose of acquiring knowledge or skill. It must contain information on a topic and instructions for a task. A Learning Center needs to include the supplies and equipment necessary to complete an assignment or activity. Learning Centers may be created in many ways. They may be constructed on tabletops, desks, counters, bulletin boards, chalkboards, walls, or any other surface that will hold the essential elements. Learning Centers may be extremely efficient, containing the bare essentials required for achieving the desired results, or extraordinarily elaborate with bountiful enhancements to supplement the anticipated outcomes.

Learning Centers create an opportunity for the learning to occur; develop discovery learning techniques; emphasize hands-on experiences; focus attention on specific topics and tasks; foster cooperative learning; promote critical thinking skills; provide self-directed, individualized instruction; release imagination and ideas.

Learning Centers may be used in virtually any educational setting. They are ideal for Church School classes, Worship centers, Children's Church, Vacation Bible School, Mid-week ministries, Kid's clubs, Intergenerational Events, Before and After School care programs, Youth Groups, Retreats, Confirmation Classes, and more. Learning Centers are for people of all ages—children, youth and adults. Designed especially for individual students, learning centers also work well for small group projects. Suggestions for adapting Learning Centers to other program designs are provided in Chapter Fourteen.

Provided in an easy-to-use format, the activities for each chapter list the materials required for the project, offer directions for advance preparation, and give complete directions for accomplishing the task. If the activity is to be used in a Learning Center, the instructions must be copied and placed in the display together with the required supplies.

Laws To Love By: The Ten Commandments is a valuable resource for anyone involved in the worship, education, outreach and nurture ministries of a congregation. It is also appropriate for use in school and home.

May all who participate in this study affirm and appreciate the Ten Commandments as God's "Laws To Love By."

CHAPTER ONE

An Introduction To The Ten Commandments

Introduce learners to a study of the Ten Commandments by using the activities in this chapter. Each of the five Learning Centers provides information and insight into a series of important questions. WHO gave the Ten Commandments and WHO received them? WHAT are they? WHEN were they given? WHERE were they given and kept, and WHERE can they be found today? WHY were they given and WHY should they be observed? Through involvement in these lessons participants will begin to understand that the answers to all five questions are related to the theme of love — love for God, self, and others.

WHO?

Materials

- ❑ Clay (Air drying)
- ❑ Rolling pin
- ❑ Table knife
- ❑ Bible
- ❑ Air tight container for unused clay
- ❑ Utility knife
- ❑ Craft sticks

Advance Preparation

- ❑ Roll the clay into small balls and place them in an air-tight container.
- ❑ Pre-sharpen the craft sticks for those who may need assistance.

Method

After God delivered the Israelites from the land of Egypt, He continued to provide for their needs in many ways. God supplied manna to eat and water to drink and led the travelers with a cloud during the day and a column of fire at night. While the Israelites were camped at Mount Sinai, God gave Moses a special message for the people. It is recorded in Exodus 19:3-6. God told the people that they would make a promise to one another, a covenant, like the promises He had once made with Abraham, Isaac, and Jacob. God and the people would promise to love one another forever. God gave the Israelites the Ten Commandments as the guidelines for loving God, themselves, and others. By keeping these laws, the people would show their love for God.

Review the three ways God gave the Ten Commandments to Moses and the Israelites. Three days after Moses met with God, thunder and lightening filled the sky, the mountain was covered with clouds and smoke, and loud trumpet blasts sounded. When the people gathered at the base of the mountain, God spoke the Ten Commandments. Later Moses climbed the mountain again to meet God, and this time God wrote the Ten Commandments on two tablets of stone. Since Moses was gone for forty days and nights, the people of Israel thought they had been abandoned. They created their own god in the form of a golden calf. On his way down the mountain, Moses saw what was taking place in the camp. He became so angry that he threw down the two tablets of stone and broke the commandments. After asking God's forgiveness, Moses was instructed to hew out two tables of stone and to return to the mountain. Once again Moses spent forty days and nights with God, and once again God gave him two tables of stone to take to the people.

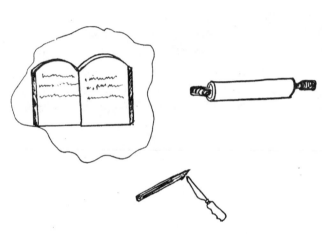

Make two tablets as a reminder of the WHO in this story. Use the symbol as a reminder of God's love for the Israelites and for us. Select a ball of clay. Roll the ball in the palms of your hands until it is pliable, and then flatten the clay into a slab about 1/2" thick. Use the rolling pin, if desired. With your fingers, or with a table knife, form the clay into the shape of two tablets of stone, representing the two stone tables of the Ten Commandments. Allow the clay to dry. Use the utility knife to sharpen one end of a craft stick to use as a writing implement. Use the stick to scratch letters into the tablets. On the left side, write ways in which God showed His love for the people of Israel. Look up Bible passages such as Exodus 12:29- 32, Exodus 14:19, and Exodus 16:13,14, as idea starters. On the right side, write ways in which God shows His love for you. Look up John 3:16 to remember one of the most important ways. Set the stone tablets in a place that will remind you of God's laws of love.

WHAT?

Materials

- ❑ Metal tray
- ❑ Index cards, 3" x 5"
- ❑ Scissors
- ❑ Envelopes
- ❑ Self-stick magnetic strips
- ❑ Pens or pencils
- ❑ Ruler
- ❑ Bible

Method

The Ten Commandments form the basis of laws and moral codes for our civilization. Think of these commandments as guidelines or sign posts directing us to "right living." The observance of the Ten Commandments began at Mount Sinai with a covenant between the Israelites and God.

In order for the "covenant people" to live and work together, they had to establish rules. God gave guidelines to them through Moses, their leader. God promises to take care of His people and to bless them. In gratitude for the Lord's blessings, the Hebrews agreed to live according to the Ten Commandments.

The Ten Commandments are listed in the Bible in Exodus 20:1-17 and again in Deuteronomy 5:1-22. Read the entire passage in either or both Exodus or Deuteronomy, then plan to memorize a shortened list, such as:

1. Put no other gods before me.

2. Worship no idols.

3. Do not take the Lord's name in vain.

4. Keep the Sabbath holy.

5. Honor your father and mother.

6. Do not murder.

7. Do not commit adultery.

8. Do not steal.

9. Do not bear false witness against your neighbor.

10. Do not covet what belongs to your neighbor.

Try this activity to help with the memorizing. Mark and cut strips from the note cards, approximately five inches by one inch. Snip one end of each card strip to represent the shape of a directional sign on a sign post. Write or print each commandment on a separate piece of cardstock. Cut a section of magnet long enough to support each "commandment" strip. Place the strips in order on the tray and say them to yourself several times.

Close your eyes and remove a strip or have someone else take away one of the pieces. Test yourself to determine if you know which commandment is missing. Another way to check your memory is to scramble the pieces on the tray, then try to put them back in proper order. Practice until you know the commandments by heart!

Label the envelope with the title and scripture references. Use the Ten Commandment magnet strips at home on a tray, metal cabinet, or refrigerator.

Moses learned about the guidelines for "right living" from God; the Israelites learned from Moses; and we have learned from the writings in the Bible. See if you can use these "sign posts" to direct or to teach another person.

WHEN?

Materials

- Bible
- Scissors
- Ruler
- Roll of paper (Adding machine tape or shelf paper)
- Pencils
- Markers
- Bible reference books

Method

The Ten Commandments have provided the foundation for laws in many parts of the civilized world. It is important to know WHEN God presented these laws or guidelines to His people; not only when in history this event took place, but also, at what point in the story of the Hebrew people.

The story of the Exodus, the "going out" of Israel from Egypt, took place more than three thousand years ago. The second book of the Bible records these very significant events of Hebrew history. It tells how God's people escaped from slavery in Egypt, wandered for years through the wilderness, and made a covenant with God at Mount Sinai. It was there that God gave His people laws instructing them how to live and how to worship.

Moses led the Israelites from Sinai to Canaan, the land that had been promised to their forefathers. As the people of Israel struggled to begin a new nation, it was important that they honored their covenant with God. It was necessary for the forming nation to obey the Ten Commandments, as well as other laws, and to place God foremost in their lives as they journeyed to the Promised Land.

Make a time line to help visualize WHEN all of this took place. Use the list of scripture references which follow or add others that you have discovered.

Creation	Genesis 1 & 2
Adam & Eve/Sin	Genesis 3 & 4
Noah/Flood	Genesis 5-9
Babel/Start of Nations & Languages	Genesis 10 & 11
Abraham/Covenant (2100 B.C.)	Genesis 17
Ishmael & Isaac	Genesis 25
Jacob/Blessing	Genesis 27
Joseph/Egypt (1900 B.C.)	Genesis 39-50
Israel/Slaves	Exodus 1
Moses/Leader	Exodus 2-4

Moses/Exodus (1450 B.C.)	Exodus 14-19
Moses/Ten Commandments (1450 B.C.)	Exodus 20-24
Tabernacle/Ark	Exodus 25-40
Victory/Moses' Death	Deuteronomy 33,34
Joshua/Promised Land (1399 B.C.)	Joshua 1-6
Heroes/Deborah, Gideon, Samson	Joshua 1-6
Kingdom/Saul, David (1043 B.C., 1000 B.C.)	I & II Samuel
Solomon/Temple (960 B.C.)	I Kings, II Chronicles
Kingdom Divides/Israel, Judah (931 B.C.)	I & II Kings
Solomon's Temple Destroyed (586 B.C.)	Jeremiah 39-52
Captivity & Return (458 B.C.)	Ezra
Jesus/Birth & Teachings (5 B.C. - 30 A.D.)	Gospels

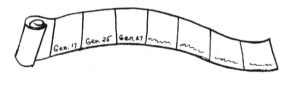

Scan through the Bible and any dictionaries, atlases or reference books available. Choose some of the stories familiar to you or select events you would like to learn about. Look through the books to get basic information from headings and pictures. If there is time, read the passages that appear interesting.

Draw pictures and symbols to represent the events you have selected. Use the ruler and pencil or marker to separate the time periods. Write in the title and date of each event. Now you can visualize the Ten Commandments place in the history of the Bible. See if you can find a time line chart to compare how this important event fits into the history of civilization.

WHERE?

Materials

- ❑ Bible
- ❑ Scissors
- ❑ Pencils
- ❑ Fabric paint
- ❑ Iron
- ❑ Fabric glue
- ❑ Sturdy fabric, such as denim, canvas, corduroy, twill or drapery fabric
- ❑ Clean up supplies
- ❑ Rulers
- ❑ Scrap paper
- ❑ Paintbrushes
- ❑ Waxed paper
- ❑ Chalk

Advance Preparation

❏ Invite each participant to bring a Bible.

❏ Set up an ironing station and recruit an adult to supervise this portion of the activity.

Method

WHERE were the Ten Commandments given to the Israelites? WHERE did the people of God enshrine the tablets of stone after making the covenant with God? WHERE can we find the Ten Commandments today?

Following God's direction, Moses led his people out of the land of Egypt, where they had been slaves. After a three-month journey through the desert, the people of Israel camped at the foot of Mount Sinai. Moses knew that before continuing on the way to the promised land, his people needed laws to live by. It was at this mountain that God gave Moses the Ten Commandments.

The Israelites stayed at Mount Sinai for nearly a year. During that time they learned about additional laws and were given instructions for building the tabernacle, a holy place to worship God. Inside the tabernacle was a gold-covered wooden chest, the Ark of the Covenant. The Ark enclosed the two stone tablets which were inscribed with the commandments.

The Ark was carefully designed to be portable, so that when it was time to leave Sinai for the land of Canaan, the Ark of the Lord led the procession. The Israelites not only enshrined the Law in the sacred chest, but they also carried God's law in their hearts.

Where can we find these important laws of God? Look in the second and fifth books of the Bible ... in Exodus 20:1-17 and in Deuteronomy 5:1-22. If you memorize the Ten Commandments and understand their meaning, you can carry God's law in your heart!

fold...
Iron to crease

Throughout history, people have wanted to embellish or to beautify the covering for the written word of God. In this activity, you will design a decorative cover for your Bible.

Choose fabric that you like; then open your Bible on top of the cloth. In order to measure the correct size, add 1-1/2 inches along the top and bottom edges of the book for a hem allowance. Extend the cloth about four inches beyond both right and left sides of the Bible to form end flaps.

Set aside the Bible until later. Proceed to the ironing area and allow an adult to help with this part of the activity. On the top and bottom edges of the fabric, fold over a "hem" approximately 1-1/2 inches (the finished height of the cloth should be just a tiny bit taller than the height of the Bible.) Iron the fabric with firm pressure and warm enough temperature to give a sharp crease along the top and bottom of the material. If the cloth does not hold a crease, use some small dots of fabric glue inside the hem, but do not fasten the four-inch flap allowance on each end of the fabric book cover.

Lay the spine of the open Bible in the center of the creased cloth. Slide the left cover of the Bible into the "pocket" formed by the folded hems; then lift the center of the book enough to slide

the right cover into the "pockets" on the other side.

On a piece of scrap paper, plan a design for the cover you have made. Consider symbols that remind you of the way Moses was given God's Law: Mount Sinai, stone tablets, clouds. Or, create any design you think will make an attractive cover.

Remove the cover from your Bible. It will be easier to paint if the cover is lying flat on the work surface. Be sure to mark with chalk or pencil where you want the painting to be. Place a piece of waxed paper under the cloth to prevent painted areas from sticking to the work surface.

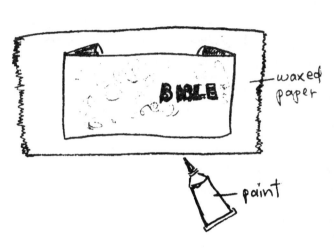

Use fabric paints in tubes or apply paint with a brush to create your design. Take care to plan and to keep the decoration simple. Too much paint may peel away or may make the Bible hard to handle. Allow the paint to dry according to directions on the tube or bottle. Now you are ready to cover your Bible!

When carrying your Bible with you, remember how important God's word was to the Israelites as they traveled to the Promised Land. Keep a bookmark at the pages where the Ten Commandments are listed.

WHY?

Materials

- ❏ Scissors
- ❏ Glue or stapler and staples
- ❏ Markers
- ❏ Felt, fabric interfacing, or construction paper
- ❏ Trims such as lace, rick rack, or buttons
- ❏ Bible

Method

All of the WHY questions related to the Ten Commandments can be summarized in one word: LOVE. God gave the Ten Commandments to the Israelites, and to us as well, out of love for His people (Exodus 19:4,5). God's people keep the Laws to show their love for God. In fact, the first four commandments are guides for expressing our love for God, and the remaining six offer directions for demonstrating our love for self and others. Jesus summarized the Ten Commandments into two: Love for God and love for self and others. Read Jesus' words in Matthew 22:37-40.

Make a pocket heart, a symbol of love, as a reminder of WHY the Ten Commandments were given and WHY they are to be kept.

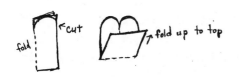

Cut the fabric or paper into 6" x 12" or 12" x 18" pieces. Fold the materials in half vertically and cut the top to a rounded shape. Unfold. Bring the bottom of the material up to the top and crease.

Next, fold the lower right and left corners toward the center and crease.

Fold the top flap of the material down and glue or staple it in place.

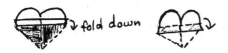

Write the word "God" on the top of the heart, "Self" on the left side, "Others" on the right side, and "Ten Commandments" on the flap. Decorate the heart with a variety of trims.

Carefully open the pocket. It can be filled with something special, such as flowers or candy. Remember that the Ten Commandments are more than just a set of rules for behavior. They are an attitude of the heart: love.

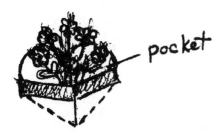

CHAPTER TWO

The First Commandment

Exodus 20:3 records the words of the first commandment: "You shall have no other Gods before me." Topping the list of ten, this "law to love by" reminds us that God the Creator, who revealed Himself through His Word and His world, is the one, the only one, to trust, obey, worship, and love. This God, rather than the variety of "gods" people revere, must have first place in our lives. Five Learning Center activities, focusing on the themes of "One" and "First," are intended to help participants gain a greater understanding of this important instruction and grasp the message that the First Commandment invites us into an intimate union with a loving God.

SINGLE MOST IMPORTANT

Materials

- Dowel rods
- Drill
- Clay
- Brushes
- Paper
- Wood pieces, 3" x 5" or 5" x 7"; one per participant
- Bibles
- Glue
- Tempera paints
- Shellac
- Pencils

Advance Preparation

- Drill holes into the centers of the wooden bases.
- Glue the dowel rods, in an upright position, into the bases.

Method

In Bible times, many people prayed to idols, or "gods," of wood or stone. They thought these objects had great power and could hear their prayers. We know that a god of wood or stone has no power, can never answer prayer, and could certainly never love anyone. But God, with a capital "G," can do all these things, for Jehovah is the one true God, the only God. Only God can hear us and help us when we pray. Only God loves and sustains us. Unfortunately, people sometimes have a hard time remembering and believing this simple truth. Take the Israelites, for example. They had just made a covenant with God: they would keep the Ten Commandments, the guides for their lives, and Jehovah would be their God forever. But while Moses was on the mountain talking with God, actually receiving the Ten Commandments, the Hebrew people became impatient and created another god, or idol—a golden calf.

Although this incident happened a long time ago, people create idols, or their own gods, everyday. Modern day idols include things like clothes, hobbies, bikes, cars, super stars, and more. An idol is something that is "worshiped" or "revered" — often more than the true and only God. Take time to think about "idols" or "gods" that may be part of your life. Are things like being on the soccer team, building a great CD collection, or buying the best bike on the top of your list? Are they more important than God?

Create a symbolic sculpture as a reminder that Jehovah is the single most important God. On a piece of paper, list some of the "gods" in your life. Think of a symbol to represent each item on the list, like a dollar sign for money or a cord for electronic devices. Using pieces of clay, sculpt these objects. Select a wooden base and attach the items to it. Mold the letters "G O D" from pieces of clay and affix them to the top of the sculpture. When the clay is dry, the sculptures may be painted and sealed with a protective coating. Set the sculpture in a special place and let it serve as a reminder that there is only one God.

ONE AND ONLY

Materials

- Wood blocks or scraps
- Water base varnish or polymer coating
- Bibles
- Heavy copy paper or parchment
- Rulers
- Erasers
- Brass, screw-type rings for picture hanging
- Sandpaper
- Small paintbrushes
- Fine-tipped markers or calligraphy pens
- Pencils
- Scrap paper
- Clean-up supplies

Method

God presented His laws to the Hebrew people emphasizing that He was the one and only God—a sovereign power. The word sovereign means supreme authority, above all others or greatest.

In many instances, the writings in the Bible explain or announce God's greatness. Psalm 8 begins and ends with the same exclamation: "O Lord, our Sovereign, how majestic is your name in all the earth!" One reason that God is so great, or the one and only, is because God created everything! Psalm 47 is a song of praise: "Clap your hands, all you peoples; shout to God with loud songs of joy. For the Lord, the Most High, is awesome, a great king over all the earth."

Read all of Psalm 8 and Psalm 47, then choose one of the verses to place on a wooden plaque using a special technique called decoupage. Select the verse that best explains the importance of God and copy it onto a piece of scrap paper; set it aside.

Cover the work space, then choose a piece of wood for the decoupage plaque. Carefully sand the front, back and edges to eliminate any rough spots. If you wish to have slightly rounded edges on the plaque, use coarse sandpaper to rub away the sharp corners. Use fine sandpaper for a smooth surface.

Brush on a water-base varnish or polymer sealer to give the wood a natural finish. Set the wood out of the way to dry where it will not be disturbed.

Cut paper into an oval or rectangular shape that will fit your wooden block. Torn edges give an interesting look to the printed material. Use a marker or calligraphy pen to letter the verse onto the paper. Refer to the verse that was copied on scrap paper. Mark light guidelines with a pencil and ruler before lettering on the heavy paper or parchment. Be sure to allow the ink to dry before continuing.

Brush a tiny bit of the polymer or varnish on the center of the wood plaque and attach the paper with the Bible verse. Brush a light coating of the finishing material over the paper and the wood. Allow to dry and add another coat, if time permits. Clean brushes thoroughly, according to directions on varnish or polymer container.

When the clear finish is completely dry, fasten a decorative hanger to the top edge of the wooden piece. A brass, screw-type ring or eyelet is sturdy and looks attractive.

Hang the decoupage plaque where you and your household can be reminded of God's greatness and of the theme of the first commandment: God is the one and only!

FIRST PLACE

Materials

- ❑ Construction paper, blue
- ❑ Stapler and staples
- ❑ Bible
- ❑ Circle pattern, three-inch
- ❑ Hole punch
- ❑ String
- ❑ Crepe paper streamers, blue
- ❑ Fine-line markers
- ❑ Gold seals or gold paper
- ❑ Glue sticks
- ❑ Scissors

Method

The Israelites agreed to live their lives according to the Ten Commandments. God gave Moses the laws to help Israel have order in their lives so they could move ahead as a great nation. God wanted the people of Israel to forget about the gods they had been worshiping and to place Him in the Number One spot! This commandment is so significant, that God put it first on the list.

Often times, the "first" is the most noticed, best remembered, or most important such as first steps, first day at school, or first bicycle. Think about the ways you like to be first: standing in line, winning a game, or finishing something before others. We feel valued when we are Number One! However, the first commandment instructs us to put God first in our life. God is more important than anything. God is Number One! Read Mark 10:17-22 to learn what Jesus said about "first place."

Make a "First Place" ribbon as a reminder of God's First Commandment. Trace and cut a circle from the blue paper. In the Bible, find Exodus 20:3 and with a marker, copy the first commandment around the edge of the blue circle. Cut a length of crepe paper about four times the distance around the circle. Gather the blue crepe paper into pleats and staple around the outside edge of the circle forming a rosette. Add on two streamers to complete the "first place" blue ribbon. Mark a large number "1" into a gold seal or gold paper circle. Glue the gold shape into the center of the rosette. If you wish to hang the blue ribbon, punch a hole at the top edge and tie on a piece of string to complete the project. Display the ribbon to remind you and others about the First Commandment: God is in First Place!

FIRST PRIORITY

Materials

- ❑ Book(s) of devotions or prayers
- ❑ Hymnal
- ❑ Pencils
- ❑ Markers
- ❑ Dictionary
- ❑ Scrap paper
- ❑ Construction paper

Method

The First Commandment teaches us to put God first in our lives and to trust only in Him. We must always remember that God provides our food, our families, our homes, and our friends. The Commandments were meant to be loving guidelines to help people live the right kind of life. It is important that we obey God's law and that we thank Him for what He has given us. One way we can thank God for all He has provided is to tell Him! Prayer is the way we talk to God.

Sometimes a prayer can be one word, it can be lots of words, or just a feeling in the heart. To help you in your conversation with God, here are four important parts of a prayer:

Adoration—praising God for His greatness;

Confession—telling God about something you did that was not following the Ten Commandments;

Thanksgiving—thanking God for His love and for His gifts;

Supplication—asking for God's help or guidance.

This activity will help you learn how to form a prayer and will remind you to put your trust in God. Spend some time skimming through books of prayers. Look up these "prayer" words in the dictionary: adoration, confession, thanksgiving and supplication. Check in the church hymnal to find songs with those "prayer" words as themes; then read the words to the hymns. This should help you begin to form your own prayer. Use the scrap paper to write down some of your ideas.

Choose a favorite color of construction paper. Fold it the short way into half, then fourths, then eighths. Open up the paper and refold it on the same creases to form steps or a fan. On the bottom step, print the word "ADORATION," and on the section above it write comments to demonstrate praise for God. On the next step print "CONFESSION," then above it enter something you need to tell God. Print "THANKSGIVING" on the third step and on the section above, list reasons to be thankful. The last step is "SUPPLICATION" and the strip above can include anything for which you need God's help.

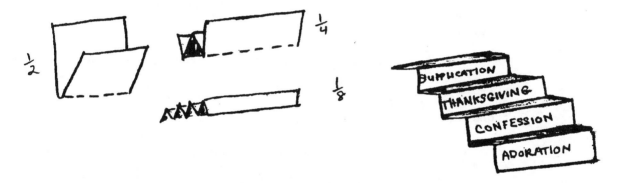

Oftentimes you might like your prayer to be private—just between you and God. In that case, just put one or two words of your personal prayer between the "prayer word" steps. Fold up the paper and use it as a bookmark or stand it up on your desk or dresser. Think about the prayer from time to time. Anytime you wish to talk to God, use the prayer step idea. Remember to trust in God; put no one or nothing before Him.

ONE GOD: THREE PERSONS

Materials

- ❏ Cube
- ❏ Fleur-de-lis
- ❏ Shamrock
- ❏ Trims like cording, braid, rick-rack
- ❏ 12" x 18" posterboard or construction paper
- ❏ Apple
- ❏ Pottery
- ❏ Glue
- ❏ Old magazines or greeting cards

Method

In the first commandment, God says "You shall have no other gods before me." Although there is one God, Christians believe that God has three ways to help us understand the Love and Light and Energy God brings to earth. We call this "The Trinity," or three-in-one concept of God: God as Father or Creator of life, God as Jesus or Redeemer of life, and God as Spirit or Sustainer of life. This does not mean we worship three Gods, but that the Trinity is a mystery we accept by faith and understand by experience.

Explore a variety of objects that will help make the idea of the Trinity seem easier to grasp.

- **Cube:** One object with three dimensions—height, width, and depth.

- **Apple :** An apple represents the Trinity in that it has three parts: the outer layer of skin, the sweet fruit, and the inner core containing the seeds.

- **Fleur-de-lis:** From French royalty comes this symbol also used as a sign of the Trinity, three flower petals, yet one flower.

- **Pottery:** A clay pot is an "earthen vessel" like human beings, a trinity created by the potter's skilled hands, the wet clay, and the power of the turning wheel.

- **Shamrock:** Legend says that Saint Patrick explained the Trinity by using the three-leafed shamrock of Ireland, pointing out that it is one plant with one stem, yet it has three separate leaves.

- **Water:** Water is two parts hydrogen and one part oxygen, yet that same chemical substance can be experienced in its liquid form or as a solid—ice, or as a vapor—steam.

- **Triangle:** While it is one distinct shape, a triangle is made of three sides.

Choose one theme to use to develop designs on a triptych. A triptych, or three fold display, is an ancient Christian art form. The triptych was used to display three pictures or images about God, and to remind people of the Trinity. Each picture or image would be displayed in a separate arched panel, yet the three panels were connected. To form the triptych, fold 12" x 18" posterboard or construction paper into thirds across the width. Create simple arches at the top of each panel. All three sections can be the same size or the center panel can be left taller. Adding gold foil paper for a background or trimming with cord, braid, or rick-rack will add an elegant touch to the triptych. Add the chosen design to each of the three panels. Separate one symbol into its parts and draw them on the different panels, or put a separate symbol on each. Another possibility would be to cut pictures from magazines or use old greeting cards to find symbols to glue on each panel. Once the design is complete, stand the triptych as a table decoration or altar display.

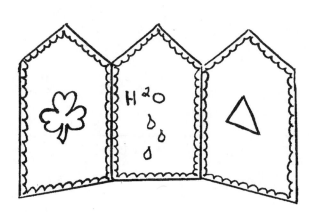

CHAPTER THREE

The Second Commandment

"You shall not make for yourself an idol, whether in the form of anything that is in heaven above, or that is on the earth beneath, or that is in the water under the earth. You shall not bow down to them or worship them; for I the Lord your God am a jealous God, punishing children for the iniquity of parents, to the third and the fourth generation of those who reject me, but showing steadfast love to the thousandth generation of those who love me and keep my commandments." (Exodus 20:4-6)

Five Learning Center activities will help participants review the Ten Commandments, recall the message of the prophets to the people of the Old Testament, remember Paul's New Testament words regarding idols, recognize God in the stories of the Bible in their own lives, and respond to keeping the Second Commandment today.

REVIEW: THE TEN COMMANDMENTS

Materials

- ❑ Tongue depressors (11 per project)
- ❑ Key ring or key chain
- ❑ Craft drill or hand drill (with smallest bit)
- ❑ Permanent markers with fine tips
- ❑ Bibles
- ❑ Scrap lumber or old cutting board
- ❑ Pencils and paper
- ❑ Sandpaper
- ❑ C-clamps
- ❑ Rubber bands
- ❑ Prepared list of Ten Commandments

Method

The Ten Commandments represent the basic rules for "right living." These rules or laws were given to us by God to guide us throughout our lifetime. It is important that we not only learn to list the Ten Commandments, but that we begin to understand them as well.

There are many ways to memorize important bits of information. One way is to repeat and review the material over and over. By the end of these lessons on the Ten Commandments, you will be able to name the commandments and will have a better understanding of the meaning of God's special laws. This project provides you with a handy learning tool to help you memorize.

Read the Ten Commandments in the Bible. (Exodus 20:1-17) Write a simple version of the list by using just the key words or refer to the list that has been prepared for you. Set the list aside for now.

Prepare eleven tongue depressors by sanding lightly and by drilling a small hole in one end of each stick. Protect the work surface with an old piece of wood or cutting board, so holes are not drilled into a table or desk! Before drilling each tongue depressor, fasten it to the board with a C-clamp to keep it from shifting. You may try clamping and drilling two at one time!

Number and print the commandments onto the wood with a fine-tipped marker, lettering one law per stick. Be certain to print neatly. Sand away any printed mistakes or any rough spots near the drilled holes. Stack the drilled, lettered tongue depressors in order. On the extra piece, print TEN COMMANDMENTS and add EXODUS 20:1-17. Slip the key ring or chain through the holes, then stretch a rubber band around the opposite end to hold the stack together.

Keep the "Laws of God" with you ... in your pocket, purse or book bag. Look at the list several times a day and before long, you will have memorized the Ten Commandments.

RECALL: OLD TESTAMENT PROPHETS

Materials

- ❏ Bibles
- ❏ Thick tempera or finger paint
- ❏ Zip-lock plastic bags

Method

An idol is a false god. People in Bible times often worshiped statues they made from wood, stone or metal. They worshiped these representations of a god instead of the true God, Jehovah. Many Old Testament passages record the role of the prophets in calling people to turn away from idols and to turn to God. Two popular stories include the account of Elijah and the Priests of Baal, I Kings 18:20-40, and Daniel and King Nebuchadnezzar, recorded in Daniel 3. Review these, and other stories of the prophets, in a unique way.

Pour thick tempera or finger paint into a self-sealing plastic bag, filling the Zip-lock container one-fourth of the way. Press out as much air as possible. Close the bag securely. Look up one of the Scripture passages, read the account, and use your fingers to "draw" picture stories on the outside of the bag. Review and remember the important message that the prophets called people to turn away from idols, or to erase them from their lives, and to only worship the one true God. After illustrating one story, erase the picture by rubbing the palm of your hand over the bag to smooth the paint.

Additional Old Testament stories to use for this project include Ezekiel 14:1-3, 6; Jeremiah 23:16-18; and Habbakuk 2:18- 20.

REMEMBER: NEW TESTAMENT STORIES

Materials

- ❑ Pencils
- ❑ Dowel rods
- ❑ Markers
- ❑ Cardboard box (any size including a tiny matchbox, a standard shoe box, or a large carton)
- ❑ Paper, sheets or roll
- ❑ Knife or scissors
- ❑ Tape
- ❑ Cardboard or wood scraps

Method

One of the followers of Jesus was Paul who became a great teacher and missionary. As he traveled, he told the people about the laws of God and the teachings of Jesus. While in Athens, Greece, Paul was disturbed to discover that the city was filled with idols.

Read the account of Paul's visit to Athens in Acts 17:16-25. Try to picture in your mind what the scenes would look like if you were illustrating a book or making a movie. Some of the scenes would include Paul's concern about idol worship as he argued with the Jews in the synagogue, talked with the devout Greeks, and lectured to other Athenians in the marketplace. View Paul having a serious conversation with philosophers who were intrigued with the information about Jesus. Paul was taken before the Areopagus, a city council whose purpose was to question teachers who lectured in public.

Imagine the scene when Paul addressed the Athenians about their objects of worship and commented on an altar inscription: "To an unknown god." He proceeded to explain that "the God who made the world and everything in it, he who is the Lord of heaven and earth, does not live in shrines made by human hands, nor is he served by human hands, as though he needed anything, since he himself gives to all mortals life and breath and all things." (Acts 17:24-25) When the crowds heard Paul's description of the Resurrection of Jesus, most of them ridiculed him, but a few became believers.

Read again the passage about Paul's experience in Athens and plan illustrations for a video box mural. Pay special attention to the facial expressions as you retell the sequence of events in picture form. Follow these instructions to fashion a video story box using a standard size shoe box. If making a smaller or larger viewer, choose rods and paper to fit. With scissors or knife, cut an opening in the center of the bottom of the box. Turn the box on its side so that the bottom becomes the front or viewing area.

Use a knife or scissor points to cut a set of parallel holes in the top and bottom on both sides of the window. Place a dowel rod through each set of holes. Keep them in place with a strip of wood or cardboard used as a stop.

Depict several events in Paul's visit to Athens by drawing with markers directly onto the paper roll or on individual sheets of paper. Leave a space between pictures if planning to use the roll of paper; if using individual pieces of paper, tape blank sheets between each drawing to form a continuous piece. You may choose to add scripture or captions in the spaces between scenes. Be sure the paper is a little wider than the viewing area.

Attach the beginning of the mural to one dowel rod and the end to the other. Wind the illustrated paper along the "screen" opening to tell the story of Paul's teachings in Acts 17. Share your video story with a friend or relative.

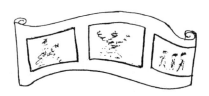

RECOGNIZE: GOD IN YOUR LIFE

Materials

- ❏ Paper
- ❏ Bibles
- ❏ 8" paper plates
- ❏ Brass fasteners
- ❏ Glue

- ❏ Pencils
- ❏ Timing device
- ❏ Construction paper
- ❏ Old magazines or church school papers
- ❏ Markers or crayons

Advance Preparation

- ❏ Prepare a sample "window" pattern.

Method

No idols! That's the message of the Second Commandment. These words remind us that our God, our great Creator, cannot be represented by or limited to a piece of wood, or stone or metal. Since we cannot portray God through an image, how do we recognize God? The answer is easy: We recognize God by what God does rather than by what God looks like.

Take a few minutes to think about the ways in which you recognize God. Select a piece of paper and fold it in half. On one half write the ways you recognize God in the lives of the people of the Bible. Stories include the Israelites and the Red Sea, Noah and the Ark, and David and Goliath. On the other half write the ways you recognize God in your own life. Think about the beauty of a mountain or a meadow, the smile of a friend or a family member, and the assurance of God's strength and support. Using a timing device, such as a stop watch or a watch with a second hand or digital read-out, time yourself for one minute as you recall Biblical events. At the end of sixty seconds, stop, and start again, timing yourself for one more minute as you recall personal themes. Set the paper aside.

Cut an 8" circle from construction paper, using a paper plate as a pattern. Find or draw pictures to illustrate ways you recognize God, through the Bible stories, and in your own life. Glue

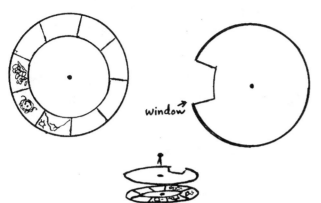

or place the pictures on the outside edge of the construction paper circle. Next, using the sample pattern, take an 8" paper plate and cut a window into it. Place the paper plate on top of the circle of pictures. Push a brass fastener through the center of both pieces to hold them together. Turn the wheel to review the ways that you recognize God in your life.

RESPOND: THE COMMANDMENT TODAY

Materials

- ❏ Bibles
- ❏ Pencils or fine-tipped markers
- ❏ Special pens for transparencies
- ❏ Tissue or paper towel
- ❏ Plain white paper
- ❏ Acetate sheets used for overhead projector transparencies
- ❏ Ruler

Method

We understand that idols are false gods made of wood, stone or precious metal, and that images can be a picture or figure of someone or something. The Bible teaches us that we cannot limit God to have the form or shape of an object made by human beings. The true and personal God of heaven sees, hears, loves and creates. A statue or picture cannot do any of those things!

Sometimes we forget that God promised to love us always and we make other persons or other things more significant than God. In our life, an idol can be whatever we consider most important. For some people, success, wealth and good times are considered blessings from God; but, for others, those conditions can become the center of life ... much like idols.

Read the Second Commandment in two places: Exodus 20:4-6 and Deuteronomy 5:8-10. Take a few minutes to think about some of the good things in your life and some of the ways you spend your time. In this activity you will have the opportunity to check what is most important to you.

Use the pencil and ruler to divide a piece of paper into thirds by drawing lines from the top of the sheet to the bottom. In the middle section, list good things in your life as well as ways you spend time. You might include hobbies like hiking and collecting; possessions such as Nintendo and CD players; accomplishments related to sports or talents; or people, including friends and heroes. After listing a variety of good aspects of your life, think about ways these interests can glorify God or ways they can detract from God or become a type of idol worship.

Form transparent overlays to help you evaluate your list. Center one acetate sheet over the written list. At the top of the right side of the sheet print ... GLORIFY. Think of ways that the items might glorify or please God; then write a brief response for each entry. Place the second transparency over the other lists and label it at the top of the left side of the sheet ... DETRACT. Write on the new transparency the ways these same things might lead you away from God.

After looking over the list, take a few minutes to thank God for His love and ask for His guidance so that every aspect of your life will glorify Him rather than detract from Him.

The Third Commandment

"You shall not make wrongful use of the name of the Lord your God, for the Lord will not acquit anyone who misuses His name." (Exodus 20:7) In the Third Commandment, we are asked to appreciate the sacredness of God. God must be glorified by our thoughts, words, and deeds. Respect for God generates respect for self, respect for others, and respect for creation. When we revere the sacredness of God in all aspects of our lives, we avoid misusing the name of God for selfish and irreverent purposes.

As a starting point for this study, review the account of the burning bush, Exodus 3:13,14, in which God revealed His name to Moses. Notice in Exodus 20:2 that God begins the Ten Commandments with the words "I Am." Continue surveying the Third Commandment by using the five Learning Center activities contained in this lesson. "Sequence" provides a review of God's laws, "Self" involves an activity using individual and Christian names, "Swearing" includes a project on the themes of cursing and oaths, "Sanctity" supplies an exercise centered on respect for God's name, and "Sincerity" concludes the study with thoughts on the Lord's Prayer.

SEQUENCE: TEN COMMANDMENT REVIEW

Materials

- ❑ Construction paper
- ❑ Scissors
- ❑ Clothesline
- ❑ Used magazines and church school papers
- ❑ Markers
- ❑ Glue
- ❑ Clip clothespins

Advance Preparation

- ❑ Provide a poster listing the Ten Commandments in order.
- ❑ Hang a clothesline in the learning center. It may be suspended between two chairs or posts.

Method

"You shall not make wrongful use of the name of the Lord your God," Commandment Three, is one of God's ten laws to love by. The first four commandments teach us ways to show our love for God and the last six give us guides for demonstrating our love for neighbors. Before starting your study of Commandment Three, take time to review all ten of God's laws.

Study the poster that lists the Ten Commandments in their proper sequence. Select ten pieces of construction paper and write one of the commandments on each sheet. Using the magazines and church school papers, find pictures and words that illustrate the commandments and attach them to each piece of paper. Mix up the ten sheets.

Review the poster until you feel that you could list the Ten Commandments in order. Turn the poster over and test your memory! Select one piece of paper at a time, read the words, and place the Commandments in the proper sequence. One way to show sequence is to clip the pictures to the clothesline. They may also be placed on a table or floor. Turn the poster over and check your answers.

SELF: RESPECT YOUR NAME

Materials

- ❏ Tacky glue
- ❏ Elastic cord
- ❏ Small crosses
- ❏ Alphabet Beads (from craft or bead shops)
- ❏ Assorted beads (can be from cast-off jewelry)
- ❏ Beading needles
- ❏ Scissors
- ❏ Egg cartons

Advance Preparation

- ❏ Purchase beads with letters of participants' first names and sort them alphabetically into egg cartons.

Method

There are many reasons that you are special, but one of the first ways to learn about you is to know your name. You have a surname which is a family name that tells who your parents are. You have a first name, sometimes called your Christian name, that is carefully picked by your parents and is declared when you are baptized. You may have a middle name that has a certain meaning or maybe your parents liked the way it fit with your other names. Everyone's name is important and should not be dishonored no matter how it was chosen or to whom it belongs.

There is another way to name you ... you are a Christian! That is a label or name you should be proud to have. Many times Christians do not have an easy time when they stand up for what they believe. Just as you would not want to do anything to bring dishonor to your family's good name, you must live your life so you do not misuse the title of Christian. One of the ways we "use God's name in vain" or wrongfully use God's name" is if our words and actions do not reflect the laws of God and the teachings of Christ. With this activity, you will fashion a wristband to wear as a means to announce your personal identity and your Christian connection, as well as being a reminder for yourself about your names.

Measure the elastic around your wrist, then add a few inches to the length to allow for tying

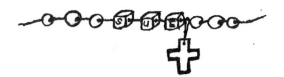

when the beads are strung. Arrange the beads on the table in front of you, placing them in the order they will appear on the finished piece. Be sure the letter beads are in the center of the row.

You may use a needle to string the beads or just cut the elastic end to a point for easier stringing. It may be necessary to trim the elastic several times to keep the point. When there are enough beads to encircle your wrist, add a cross charm or make a cross from tiny beads. Allow for ample stretch over your hand before tying the ends. To finish, tie several firm knots and add a little tacky glue to hold the closure. Trim off any extra elastic. Wear your wristband to inform others of your name and your identity as a Christian.

SWEARING: CURSES AND OATHS

Materials

- ❑ Dictionary
- ❑ Permanent markers
- ❑ Scissors
- ❑ Metal or plastic juice can lids
- ❑ Magnetic strips
- ❑ Glue

Method

Many people concentrate on only one meaning of the Third Commandment: Swearing. When they read the words "Thou Shalt not take the name of the Lord thy God in vain" they think that it refers to profanity. After you have finished the five Learning Center activities you will realize that there are several interpretations of the Third Commandment, and that "swearing" is only one of them.

Look up the word "swear" in the dictionary. Write down its two meanings. One definition is to use profane language or to curse, and the second is to make a solemn promise, or vow, with an appeal to God to confirm it.

When a person "swears" in the sense of using profanity and cursing, it dishonors God's name. God's name should only be spoken with reverence. Sometimes "swear" words are used as emphasis; to make a strong statement. "Swear" words actually detract from the statement. Taking an oath or making a vow is a different kind of swearing. When a person swears, such as in court, he or she calls on God as a witness to the truth of the statement. In both cases we must respect God's name so that God will be glorified by our thoughts, words, and actions.

To help you remember what the Third Commandment says about "swearing," or using strong words, make a magnet — a strong force — to attach to a place where you will often see it. Use a metal or plastic juice can lid as the base. With permanent markers, write the following phrases on the lid:

God's Name
Speak it with respect
Pray it with reverence
Call upon it with love

Cut a small piece of the magnetic strip and glue it to the back of the lid. Hang the magnet in a special place.

SANCTITY: RESPECT GOD'S NAME

Materials

- ❑ Paintboxes
- ❑ Paper
- ❑ Artgum or kneaded eraser
- ❑ Water
- ❑ Permanent, fine-tipped markers

- ❑ Pencils
- ❑ Scissors
- ❑ Bibles, versions used in your church
- ❑ Heavy watercolor paper or posterboard

Method

The Third Commandment is written a little differently in various versions of the Bible: "Thou shalt not take the name of the Lord thy God in vain" (King James), "You shall not misuse the name of the Lord your God" (NIV), or "You shall not make wrongful use of the name of the Lord your God" (NRSV). They all mean the same thing: we must respect God's sacredness and the holiness of His name. See if you can find any other versions of the Bible to compare phrases. Sometimes reading words expressed in more than one way will make the meaning clearer. God is sacred and we should not use His name for the wrong reasons, such as excuses for war, hatred, injustice or lies. Sometimes people will claim that God told them to do things that our God of love, trust and mercy would never consider. Throughout the Bible, writers refer to the great, holy and sacred nature of God and His name. There are many Psalms that praise in highest terms the name of God. Read Psalm 145 in any Bibles you have available and choose the one version which is the most meaningful to you. The Psalm begins with "I will extol you, my God and King, and bless your name forever and ever," and ends with "My mouth will speak the praise of the Lord, and all flesh will bless his holy name forever and ever." (NRSV)

Create a triptych illustrating this song of praise. A triptych is a picture in three parts. Fold a rectangle (12" by 18" or smaller) into thirds. While the thirds are still folded, lightly draw a point or arch shape at the top of the page. Cut on the lines and open the rectangle; the triptych should now have three sections, each with an arched top. The two end flaps may be trimmed so the center is prominent. On the left side, print or write Psalm 145:1 and on the right side copy Psalm 145:21. In the center portion lightly sketch your interpretation of Psalm 145. After reading the Psalm, images may come to mind or you may wish to express the feeling or the words by painting with water colors.

Allow the triptych to dry. Gently erase pencil lines with art gum or kneaded eraser. Use the finished piece for a private worship area to create a sacred space in your room.

SINCERITY: THE LORD'S PRAYER

Materials

- Bible
- Scissors
- Crewel or darning needles
- Embroidery hoops
- Scratch paper
- Pictures of traditional samplers
- Burlap or monk's cloth
- Yarn
- Chalk
- Dowels or sticks
- Pencils
- Embroidery "how-to" chart from craft magazine or book

Method

Reverence for God and for what He has created is the foundation for the Ten Commandments. The Third Commandment instructs us to use God's name with respect and sincerity. Jesus considered this law to be so important that he included it near the beginning of a prayer he taught his disciples ... The Lord's Prayer: "Our Father, who art in Heaven, hallowed be Thy name ..." You may know this prayer by heart, but do you know what the word hallowed means? The dictionary says "to make sacred or holy; honored." Jesus gave all of his followers this simple way to speak to God, with a built-in reminder that God's name is to be glorified. Because God and His name are truly hallowed and sacred, our prayers and any references to Him must be honorable. Sometimes memorized prayers can become rote and lack sincerity if we do not think about meanings of the words and if we do not worship with genuine feeling. Learn the meanings of the words in The Lord's Prayer so you can pray with understanding and sincerity.

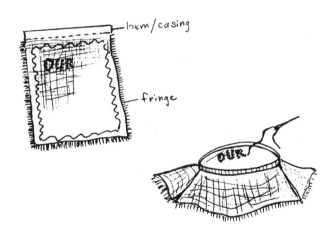

Stitch a sampler with the words, "Hallowed be Thy Name," as a reminder to honor God's name. Cut a rectangle of burlap 12" x 18". Prepare it by fringing three sides and by forming a hem or casing at the top. Look over the samples of pictures of samplers; then use scratch paper to design lettering and a border for your project. When the design is ready, redraw the plans with chalk onto the burlap. Use brightly-colored yarn and an embroidery needle to stitch along the line drawings and letters. Follow the instructions shown on a "how-to" chart to form cross stitches, running stitches, chain stitches or outline stitches. It may be helpful to try some of the stitches on a scrap of cloth before beginning the sampler. Choose the techniques that will look best with your design. Stitch carefully along the chalk lines until the sampler is complete. Sewing will be easier and stitches will be smoother if you use an embroidery hoop to keep burlap taut. Insert the dowel or stick into the casing. Add yarn to the rod so the sampler may hang as a small banner. Display your handiwork for all to see as a reminder to keep God's name holy!

CHAPTER FIVE

The Fourth Commandment

"Remember the sabbath day, and keep it holy. Six days you shall labor and do all your work. But the seventh day is a sabbath to the Lord your God; you shall not do any work - you, your son or your daughter, your male or female slave, your livestock, or the alien resident in your towns. For in six days the Lord made heaven and earth, the sea, and all that is in them, but rested the seventh day; therefore the Lord blessed the sabbath day and consecrated it." (Exodus 20:8-11)

Five Learning Center activities are offered as a way to help participants explore and experience the theme of the fourth commandment. "Do" provides an exercise to review the Ten Commandments and to put the fourth law into context; "Day" presents an explanation of the meaning of the word sabbath and discusses the difference between Saturday and Sunday observance; "Direction" points out Old and New Testament Scripture passages that relate to this guideline; "Devotion" prompts the participant to discover ways to deepen his or her relationship with God; "Different" proposes ideas for taking time to refresh body, mind and spirit. Use this program design as a way to remind the learners that observing the Fourth Commandment is another way to remember God's love for us and to show our love for God.

DO

Materials

- ❑ Bibles
- ❑ Yarn, string or shoelaces
- ❑ Corrugated cardboard squares, 8-1/2" x 8-1/2"
- ❑ Markers
- ❑ Push pins, twenty per project

Method

Learning the key points of the Ten Commandments is one way to use God's law as a guide for living. Take time to review all Ten Commandments before beginning a specific study of Commandment Four.

Choose a cardboard square and one or more markers. On the left side of the cardboard list the Commandments, underneath each other by number, beginning with Commandment One and ending with Commandment Ten. Place a push pin at the end of each line. On the right side of the square, in random order, list a key word or phrase for each commandment found in Exodus 20 or Deuteronomy 5. At the beginning of each line, place a push pin. Now, try to match the number of

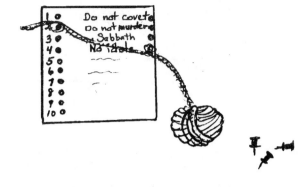

the Commandment with its key words. Using string, yarn, or shoelaces, attach a piece, approximately 10" - 20" long, to each push pin on the left side of the game board. Beginning with Commandment One, connect the piece of string to the push pin next to the key words that describe this law. Continue this procedure for each of the Commandments.

When the activity is completed, unwind the string and invite a family member or friend to try the exercise.

DAY

Materials

☐ Construction paper   ☐ Rulers
☐ Scissors   ☐ Pens
☐ Pattern

Advance Preparation

☐ Cut construction paper into 4-1/2" x 12" pieces; one per person.

☐ Cut 4" x 2" pieces of construction paper; seven per person.

☐ Duplicate "Sabbath Symbol" patterns.

Method

Sabbath means a day of rest ordained by God; in the Jewish tradition, the seventh day, Saturday; in the Christian tradition, the first day of the week, Sunday. In Genesis 2:2,3 we read that God created the world and everything in it, and rested the seventh day. In Old Testament times, people choose the seventh day, Saturday, the last day of the week, as their day of rest and worship. Since Jesus' resurrection occurred on a Sunday, Christians changed the day of rest and worship to the first day of the week. On this special day, Sunday, we praise God for our salvation!

Though the Sabbath, whether observed on Saturday or Sunday, is a special time, every day is the Lord's Day. We should try to serve God, to worship, praise, and pray, seven days a week. Make a "Sabbath Symbol" as a way to help you remember to take "Sabbath" time every day.

Select one 4-1/2" x 12" piece of construction paper. Fold the long paper into thirds, with four inches in each section. Using the pattern provided, cut two vertical slits in the center section of the strip. The slits should be 2-1/4" long and 3" apart. Fold the paper on the dotted lines indicated on the pattern. The "Weekly Worship Reminder" should now be triangular shaped. Glue the tab in place at the bottom of the paper.

Choose seven pieces of paper 4" x 2". Using a pen, write one day of the week, Sunday through Saturday, in the left-hand corner of each piece. Next, write one way to have Sabbath time

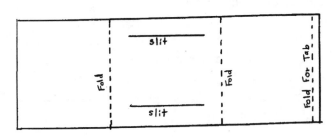

each day. Think of ways to worship and to refresh yourself physically, emotionally, and spiritually. For example, study a Scripture passage, listen to recorded music, take a walk, or share time with a family member or friend. Write one idea on each strip of paper. Insert the seven slips in order, with Sunday at the top, into the center section of the "Worship Reminder."

Take the "Sabbath Symbol" home and use it in the following way. On Sunday, follow the first suggestion. Remove the slip and place it on the bottom. Use the second idea on Monday, now at the top, and continue in this manner every day of the week. At the end of seven days, the first strip, Sunday, will again be at the top of the reminder. At this point, repeat the process.

DIRECTION

Materials

- ❑ Posterboard
- ❑ Pencils
- ❑ Scissors
- ❑ String
- ❑ Bible
- ❑ Ring, such as an embroidery hoop, plastic lid or cardboard strip fastened into a circle

- ❑ Arrow pattern
- ❑ Ruler
- ❑ Hole punch
- ❑ Markers
- ❑ Tape and stapler, optional

Method

The ways of God are good for us and the Ten Commandments provide the basic directions we need to live our lives as God intended. The Fourth Commandment instructs us to "remember the sabbath and to keep it holy." God's order includes a time for rest and worship every seven days.

There is a great deal written in the Bible about the sabbath. Right in the very beginning of the Bible, the Creation Story tells of God setting aside a sacred time for rest on the seventh day. (Genesis 2:2-3) As laws were formed, the people of Israel were supposed to remember that God had created the whole earth and that He had set them free from slavery in Egypt. The next time the sabbath appears in the scriptures is in Exodus 16:13-30, when God provided "manna" — bread from heaven — for two days, so the Israelites would not have to labor to gather food on the seventh day. Also read the Fourth Commandment as it is written in Exodus 20:8 and in Deuteronomy 5:12.

Some of the beautiful poetry and songs in the Bible give us directions on how to keep the sabbath holy. Read Psalm 92, especially verses 1-4 and Isaiah 58:13-14.

During the time that Jesus was teaching, the sabbath rules had become so complicated that he needed to remind followers of the special day's purpose: "The sabbath was made for humankind, and not humankind for the sabbath." Read in the New Testament about some of the problems Jesus had when he was helping the people understand sabbath laws. (Matthew 12:1-4 and Mark 2:23- 27) Create a mobile that includes directions for observing the sabbath. Add one of the poetry selections from Psalms or Isaiah to memorize or use as a sabbath prayer.

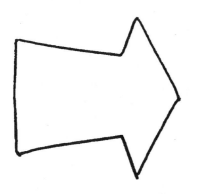

Trace and cut out three, four or five arrow shapes. Be certain to make the arrows short and "squat" instead of too thin, so they can accommodate the written information! Read the Bible passages concerning the sabbath and record the chapter and verse on one side of the arrow, write key words from each selected verse or draw symbols to illustrate the sections! Write "The Fourth Commandment" on one of the arrows and on the reverse side put "Remember the sabbath day, and keep it holy."

Punch a hole near the top of each arrow, above the writing, then attach strings. Vary the length of the strings and tie, tape or staple them to the ring. Adjust the arrows and strings so the mobile is balanced. Hang the finished project where you can be reminded to observe the sabbath.

DEVOTION

Materials

- ❑ Cardboard
- ❑ Scissors
- ❑ Colored tissue paper
- ❑ Brush
- ❑ Black permanent marker
- ❑ Tape

- ❑ Pencils
- ❑ Heavy duty aluminum foil
- ❑ Cup for polymer
- ❑ Water
- ❑ Table cover
- ❑ Glossy acrylic polymer (from art or craft supply store)

Method

With the institution of the Fourth Commandment, God has given human beings an exceptional gift—a joyous and holy day of rest. One of the reasons for the sabbath day is to deepen relationships with God and others. In order to keep this commandment, God wants us to devote part of the day to Him. One of the ways we spend time with God is to worship in a group or in private.

Worship involves love, admiration, awe, reverence and adoration. We participate in a variety of activities when we worship: listen to sermons, say prayers, sing hymns, read scripture, give offerings and share communion. Sometimes, we may observe baptisms or weddings as well as other special worship services. When we do these things together we share God's love and His presence within the community of faith.

Sometimes you can visit with God or feel very worshipful when you are alone. Worship is a way to show our appreciation for God — who He is and what He has done. Although the Fourth Commandment instructs us to set apart one day for worship and rest, you may choose to have every day the Lord's Day. Set aside a quiet time to become closer to God and to pray for friends and family.

Arrange a small worship spot in your room - a place with your Bible, a plant, a special picture, or a cross. From time to time add something you create as a reminder to reserve a portion of your day or week to deepen your relationship with God.

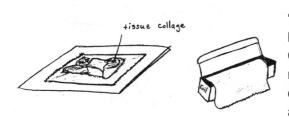

tissue collage

Design a small, decorative "stained glass window" to brighten your worship center. Cover the work area with newspaper or a plastic table cloth. Tear off a rectangle, approximately nine inches by eleven inches, of heavy duty foil and smooth it out in front of you. Tear or cut up the tissue paper. Pour a little gloss into the cup and thin with a small amount of water. Arrange tissue pieces on the foil and brush the glossy acrylic polymer all over, letting it soak through the paper. When the polymer dries, the surface of the paper will shine. Allow foil to show through here and there for colorful and dazzling results.

Cut a piece of cardboard into an arched "church window" shape. When the polymer dries, wrap the colorful foil around the cardboard form. Tape the excess foil to the back of the window shape. Complete the window by drawing "leading lines" with the black marker. You may want to draw a frame around the outside edge of the window to give it a finished look.

Cut a strip of cardboard about two inches by ten inches. Form a triangle and tape it to the back of the stained glass window for support. Enjoy the colors as you plan to worship and to keep the sabbath.

DIFFERENT

Materials

- ❑ Small, zipper type plastic bags (4 per banner)
- ❑ Scissors
- ❑ Small rod (dowel, pencil or skewer)
- ❑ Bible
- ❑ Stapler and staples
- ❑ Ribbon
- ❑ Pen or pencil
- ❑ Patterns for hand, heart and cross

- ❑ Assorted transparent and translucent materials (clear plastic pieces, colored cellophane, acetate sheets, tissue paper, giftwrap)
- ❑ Permanent markers
- ❑ Transparent tape

Method

The Fourth Commandment directed the Israelites to follow their six days of work with a day of rest. This pattern can be traced back to the Creation when God formed the earth in six days and rested on the seventh. God shows His concern for all aspects of our lives—our well-being and happiness as well as our "right living." He planned for this day to be different from our daily routine, a day to refresh body, mind and spirit.

The Bible instructs people to refrain from working, traveling or talking idly on the sabbath. This was intended to be a time set aside for worshipping God and enjoying families. In Old Testament times, families visited local shrines where they offered a sacrifice and were taught by a priest. In New Testament time, the sabbath featured a special meal on Friday evening and a visit to the synagogue to hear the law explained by a rabbi—or teacher.

Jesus taught that the sabbath was intended to benefit people. After the resurrection of Jesus, His followers began worshipping on Sunday, which was known as the Lord's Day. Many Christians now worship on Sunday, the first day of the week; however, some traditions still follow the "seventh day sabbath," and offer Saturday services.

Whatever the tradition, God intended for us to do something DIFFERENT on the sabbath. What does your family do to honor the sabbath: Go to church? Have a family dinner or gathering? Dress up? Visit friends? Think about ways you can follow God's plan to refresh yourself physically, mentally or emotionally, and spiritually: Play out of doors, learn something new, memorize a Bible verse.

Assemble a "different" kind of banner to highlight the sabbath. It should include symbols for body, mind and spirit. Choose several colors of the transparent or translucent Materials. Trace or draw your own symbols for a hand, a heart and a cross—a little smaller than the width of the plastic bag. Place one symbol inside each baggie; center, then secure with a tiny piece of tape. With the permanent marker directly on the bag or on a strip of the "see-through" material, write "Remember the sabbath day, and keep it holy" or "Body, Mind, and Spirit." Press out any air and "zip" the bag shut. Tape the top section to the rod; then tape or staple the other bags together one under the other. Tie narrow ribbon to each end of the rod and tie the two ends into a knot. Add a few more strands of ribbon to add color to your "baggie banner." Hang the banner in a window so the light will shine through the symbols and so you will keep in mind the ways God has planned for the sabbath day to be different.

CHAPTER SIX

The Fifth Commandment

"Honor your father and your mother, so that your days may be long in the land that the Lord your God is giving you. (Exodus 20:12) Review the theme of the Fifth Commandment, and make its message relevant for today by using the activities supplied for five learning centers. "History" provides a creative writing exercise to put the laws into a positive perspective; "Honor" proposes an explanation for the term, or word, as a foundation for family life; "Household" promotes respect for all caregivers through involvement in a bulletin board project; "Heritage" prompts participants to play a game researching Biblical families; and "Heirs" presents an activity depicting ways to display love, honor, and respect from generation to generation.

Through the use of the five learning centers, help the participants apply the message of the Fifth Commandment as a guide for loving God and others.

HISTORY

Materials

- ❑ Bible
- ❑ Pencils and erasers
- ❑ Markers
- ❑ Dictionary
- ❑ Posterboard

- ❑ Scratch paper
- ❑ Ruler
- ❑ Scissors
- ❑ Thesaurus
- ❑ Heavy white, manila or gray drawing paper; two sheets per person

Method

The Ten Commandments help us live our lives according to God's plan. The first four teach us how to show respect for our Creator; the remaining six instruct us how to live in harmony with other people.

At the time Moses received the Ten Commandments from God, it was essential for the Hebrew people to have guidelines to follow. Strong family life was an important foundation for the new nation. Honoring parents was listed before the laws against murdering, stealing or lying! It is just as important today to show respect for parents as well as others entrusted with our upbringing or caregiving.

Did you notice anything different about the Fifth Commandment? It is the only commandment written in a positive way; it does not include "You shall not" anywhere in the verse. In some cases, it is easier to remember and to follow a rule that is stated in a positive manner. For example, a rule at school might be: "Walk quietly" instead of "No running in the halls," and at home: "Try to get along with your brother," instead of "Don't argue with your brother." Can you think of other examples?

Read the complete list of the Ten Commandments in Exodus 29:1-17 or in Deuteronomy 5:1-22. Think about another way to state the commandment without the "you shall nots." Try out several possibilities on the scratch paper. Use reference books to help with spelling and other word choices.

Cut the top of the paper into a curved shape to represent the "stone tablets." When you have reworded the list, print each entry neatly onto the heavy paper. You may need a ruler to assist in drawing light pencil guidelines for each line of lettering. Copy five commandments on one piece of paper and the other five on the second sheet. Double check spelling, then trace over the letters with a marker.

Can you memorize the Ten Commandments? Share your rewritten, positive list with parents or friends.

HONOR

Materials

- ☐ Bible
- ☐ Pencils
- ☐ Any type of building blocks: Legos, wooden blocks, boxes, bricks
- ☐ Tape
- ☐ Paper strips (in proportion to size of blocks selected)

Method

God's purpose in commanding that we honor mothers and fathers was to establish a family unit to serve as a base for our growth and development. God planned for parents to have authority over the moral and spiritual training of their offspring. A covenant is formed when fathers and mothers accept caretaking responsibilities for every child they bring into the world and when, in return, children give respect and honor to their parents.

There are two kinds of foundations in your home: one forms the solid footing for your house - usually concrete blocks or poured concrete - and the other forms the durable base upon which your family is established. Both types of foundations have to be strong and sure! Just as builders construct with good materials on a firm base, parents help to shape children's lives with in-formation about "right living."

One of the best "tools" parents can use to build a family strong in the faith is the Holy Bible. There are many helpful verses of scripture that apply to training children and honoring parents. Complete this activity using building blocks and scripture to form a simple model of a "firm foundation."

Clear a space on the floor or table to assemble whatever type of construction you want:

house, tower, wall, cube or free- form shape. From experience you know that the foundation has to be sturdy or the structure will topple over or fall apart.

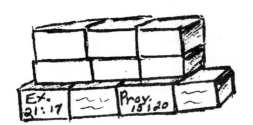

When you are done with the construction part of the activity, look up the following scripture passages to help you understand the roles of parents and children in the family: Exodus 20:12; Proverbs 15:20; Exodus 21:17; Proverbs 23:22; Leviticus 19:3; II Corinthians 12:14; Deuteronomy 5:16; Ephesians 6:1-5; Proverbs 1:8; Colossians 3:20,21; Proverbs 4:1. Many times parents guide children by teaching them verses from the Book of Psalms ... excellent "tools" for building a strong foundation. Read all of Psalm 23; Psalm 25:4,5; and all of Psalm 121.

Copy the references onto strips of paper and tape them at various spots around the base of your structure as symbols of the foundation built on "honor."

Display your work and be able to explain about the Bible verses. Select one of the verses or Psalms that is especially meaningful to you ... then memorize it. Honor your Mother and Father by reciting what you have learned!

HOUSEHOLD

Materials

- ❑ Stapler or tacks
- ❑ Scissors
- ❑ Pre-printed "coupons"
- ❑ Colored construction paper
- ❑ Photo supplies (optional)
- ❑ Markers or crayons

- ❑ Drawing paper
- ❑ Envelopes
- ❑ Pens or pencils
- ❑ Ruler
- ❑ Glue stick or photo mounting corners
- ❑ Posterboard (or space on the classroom and/or family bulletin board)

Advance Preparation

- ❑ Copy "coupon" form that can be photo-copied. Use words suggesting activities which show honor such as: hugs, chores, prayers or some specific need, to create a variety of coupons.

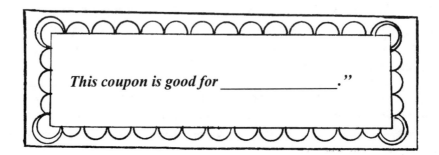

This coupon is good for _____."

Method

Our parents are partners with God in creating us; thus, the Fifth Commandment directs us to honor fathers and mothers. When we honor our parents, we show respect for God as well. God's plan is for parents to care for the little ones they bring into the world until the children are grown up and can care for themselves. Eventually, adult children need to take care of elderly parents and grandparents. God expects us to honor parents or caregivers throughout our lifetime.

In some cases, other people take the place of parents in our household or family. These guardians, similarly, deserve honor and respect. Who are the people in your household? Who are the rest of the people in your family that do NOT live in your home? What are ways you can demonstrate honor within your family unit?

Celebrating Mother's Day, Father's Day and Grandparent's Day should remind us to show devotion to these special people everyday! Create a bulletin board display or poster that can be a reminder for your household to follow the Fifth Commandment all year long.

Think about any people in your household who are responsible for you. It might be fun to include grandparents and great- grandparents, even if they are not a part of your own household. What are some of the unique characteristics of each person? On separate pieces of paper, draw portraits or action pictures to identify the individuals to be honored. Mount each drawing on a piece of construction paper with enough margin around the edges to form a colorful frame. Glue the portraits to the posterboard. If making a bulletin board display, fasten pictures with staples or tacks. Under each picture attach an envelope with the name of the person depicted. Place the envelope with the flap up so you can see the opening. Add a larger envelope at the bottom and fill it with a variety of coupons. Draw out one coupon, read what it says, and select the person who will receive your special attention. Write your name on the paper and slip the coupon in the correct envelope. Plan to do what the coupon suggests some time during the week. If you cannot hug great-grandmother because she lives far away, you can send her a "hug" in the form of a note.

Take your Fifth Commandment project home to share with your family. Once a week, perhaps on Sunday, encourage each "child" (which should include Moms and Dads with living parents and grandparents!) to pull a coupon from the larger envelope. After reading and signing the paper, they may choose a person to honor by placing the coupon in the appropriate envelope.

Next week repeat the activity, but when you draw out your slip of paper, choose a different person to honor. After several weeks, all of the envelopes will contain a few coupons. When all have been signed and the promises fulfilled, place the coupons back in the large envelope to be used again or you may wish to create new ones. Of course, you will want to honor these special people everyday ... but this will be something a little extra to think about!

HERITAGE

Materials

- ❑ "Families of Faith" game
- ❑ Paper
- ❑ Bibles
- ❑ Pencils
- ❑ Duplicating equipment
- ❑ Bible dictionary and concordance

Advance Preparation

❑ Duplicate one copy of the game sheet for each participant.

Method

Mothers and Fathers, as well as other caregivers, have the opportunity, as well as the obligation, of passing on the stories of salvation history to their children. In the Old Testament, as well as the New Testament, there are many accounts of ways in which parents shared their faith with their offspring. Review these Biblical family units by playing a matching game. Names in the column on the left side of the page are mothers and fathers, or caregivers, and names in the right-hand column are children. Draw a line from the parents to their child. Use a Bible dictionary or concordance to find additional information about each person. Also use these reference books to discover where these stories are recorded in Scripture. Look up some of the passages and read more about the heritage that has been shared through the ages.

FAMILIES OF FAITH GAME

Draw a line from the names of the parents, listed on the left, to their child, listed on the right.

1. Jacob & Rachel	A. David
2. David & Bathsheba	B. Isaac
3. Abraham & Sarah	C. Jesus
4. Obed & Wife	D. Manasseh
5. Ruth & Boaz	E. Timothy
6. Eunice & Lois	F. Solomon
7. Noah & Wife	G. Jacob
8. Saul & Wife	H. Obed
9. Mary & Joseph	I. Ham
10. Jesse & Wife	J. Cain
11. Isaac & Rebekah	K. Moses
12. Elizabeth & Zechariah	L. Jesse
13. Hezekiah & Wife	M. Joseph
14. Adam & Eve	N. John The Baptist
15. Jocabed & Husband	O. Jonathan

HEIRS

Materials

- ❑ Fabric
- ❑ Sewing equipment
- ❑ Backing material, optional
- ❑ Permanent markers or liquid embroidery pens
- ❑ Scissors
- ❑ Pencils
- ❑ Paper

Advance Preparation

- ❑ Cut a 4" x 4" or larger fabric square per person, or 26 squares if the "ABC" theme is used for the project.

Method

Look up the word "heir" in the dictionary. An heir is someone who inherits something, generally something special and significant. Through observance of the Fifth Commandment, God intends for children to "inherit" the story of His love as parents pass this "heritage" from generation to generation. Children, referred to in Commandment Five, refers to people of all ages, from the newborn baby to the elderly adult. "Children" are instructed to honor their mother and father, regardless of the age of either party. This Law spans from one generation to the next. Children who see their parents giving respect, honor and love to their grandparents, will tend to give appreciation, acclaim, and admiration to their parents as the generations mature. Honor, respect, and love, first for God and then for others, is the basis of the Fifth Commandment.

In many families, a quilt is a special gift that is inherited, or passed from one generation to the next. Make a quilt to illustrate ways that children of all ages can show honor to their parents, or caregivers. Create the blocks of the quilt individually and combine them to complete the finished product.

Use a theme for the quilt that relates to the topic of honoring family members. Create a block for every letter of the alphabet, each suggesting a way in which givers and receivers of care can show love to each other. Each square could contain a letter of the alphabet, a word or phrase related to the theme that begins with the letter, and a drawing to illustrate the topic. Some examples include:

A - Activities

B - Bake

C - Call

D - Drive

E - Example

F - Faith

G - Give

H - Help

I - Interest

J - Justice

K - Kindness

L - Love

M - Memories

N - Needs

O - Opinions

P - Plans

Q - Questions

R - Respect

S - Self Esteem

T - Talk

U - Use

V - Value

W - Work

X - Xtra

Y - Yes

Z - Zillions

A "sign-up" sheet in the Learning Center would help participants know which letters and themes have already been illustrated.

Once the themes have been identified, choose one or more of the letters to illustrate. Regardless of the subject selected, the process for completing the project is the same. Select a patch and the supplies needed to decorate it. Use drawings, symbols and words. Once the square is completed, leave it in the Learning Center for others to see.

After the squares are constructed, sew them together. This portion of the project should be done on a sewing machine by an adult or older youth. Back the piece, if desired. Display the completed project in a prominent place to remind people of the many ways in which family members can honor each other.

The Sixth Commandment

"You shall not kill." Four simple words — the Sixth Commandment found in Exodus 20:13 — with a very complex meaning! Killing, or murder — the word used in some versions of the Bible — involves more than the physical act of taking a life: it includes thoughts, words, and deeds. Killing takes many forms from homicide to holocaust, starvation to suicide, and combat to capital punishment. Use the five learning center based activities contained in this article to begin a study of the Sixth Commandment. "Illustrate" reviews all ten commandments; "Image" reminds participants of the reason for the sacredness of life; "Instruction" considers Old and New Testament teachings on the topic; "Individual" explores ways to take responsibility for actions and attitudes; "Issues" involves learning more about organizations that support life. In all of the activities remind the participants of Lewis Smedes' words in his book <u>Mere Morality: What God Expects From Ordinary People</u> (Grand Rapids, MI: Eerdmans, 1983, p. 106): "We must see every person as someone who lives each moment in relationship with God ... the one whom God made, whom God loves, whose life is in God's hands, and for whom His Son died on the cross."

ILLUSTRATION

Materials

- ❑ White drawing paper
- ❑ Cardboard
- ❑ Markers
- ❑ Old magazines
- ❑ Hole punch
- ❑ Bible

- ❑ Construction paper
- ❑ Patterns for the "Tablets of the Law"
- ❑ Pencils
- ❑ Glue
- ❑ Yarn, ribbon or string

Advance Preparation

- ❑ Prepare "Tablets of the Law" pattern(s).

Method

One, two, three, four, five, six ... It is easy to remember the numbers and to memorize the words associated with the Ten Commandments. It is harder to understand what God's laws really

Tablet pattern

mean and to apply this message to our lives today. Before beginning a study of the Sixth Commandment, review all ten statements and illustrate their meaning in the form of a shape book. Read the Ten Commandments in Exodus 20 and Deuteronomy 5. Create a shape book to illustrate the Ten Commandments. Select ten sheets of white drawing paper for the pages of the book and two pieces of colored construction paper for the front and back covers. Using the "Tablet" pattern and a pencil or marker, trace the design onto the twelve pieces of paper. Cut out the shapes. Using markers and magazine pictures, create an illustration for each commandment on a different sheet of paper. Write the number, scripture reference, or words of the commandment on the page. Design a front and back cover for the book.

Punch two holes at the top of each page and tie the papers together with string, yarn or ribbon. Share your ideas with others by leaving the shape book in the learning center until the end of the session.

IMAGE

Materials

- ❏ Tempera or acrylic paints
- ❏ Clean up supplies
- ❏ Clothesline with clothespins (or any other arrangements for drying prints)
- ❏ Good quality white construction or drawing paper
- ❏ Paintbrushes

Method

We learn at an early age that only God is great enough to originate life and that human beings are the most valuable part of His plan. The Scriptures teach that God intended for persons to be responsible for all of creation. (Genesis 1:26) Because God has granted the gift of life, we must treat all living things with respect.

The Sixth Commandment instills in us that it is wrong to destroy the precious gift of life, whether it is our own or that of someone else. God's plan is that we live without fear of having our life taken away by another person. We must care for each other.

The Bible also tells us that we are created in the likeness or image of God. (Genesis 1:27) It is stated in Psalm 8:5 that He has made mortals "a little lower than God and crowned them with glory and honor." That points out just how important we are to God. Life is sacred!

To be made in God's image means to show a likeness, to reflect or to closely resemble. Do you think that means we are similar to God in our physical appearance or in our spiritual characteristics?

Experiment with a printmaking technique that demonstrates mono-prints ... a type of print that resembles an image, but does not duplicate it exactly. The image is the same, but is less detailed and has less vivid color.

Prepare the work area and the printmaking supplies. Fold the paper in half and try your hand at painting landscapes, people, still-life arrangements or designs on the top portion of the paper, above the crease. Carefully fold up the bottom part of the paper so it covers the painted surface.

Press firmly until the paper sticks to the wet paint, then rub fingers gently across the folded piece so painted area will transfer to the blank portion. Peel back the folded-over section to reveal the reflection or repeat image picture.

Fold up for mono-print

This is called a mono-print because you are making just one copy of your original plan. The print will probably not be as distinct or as brightly colored, but it will feature the same image. This can serve as a reminder that although we are a copy of God's likeness, we can never be exactly the same.

Try several of the reflection mono-prints. Put them aside until they dry. Create an exhibit of your artistic achievements!

INSTRUCTION

Materials

- ❑ Paper
- ❑ Bible
- ❑ Thesaurus
- ❑ Pencils
- ❑ Dictionary

Method

The Sixth Commandment and the ones that follow it establish moral instruction or guidelines for getting along with the people around us. We are advised to respect and to support life, not to destroy it.

The Bible is sometimes called an instruction book for the right way to live. Moral guidance is provided for us many places in Scripture. In Psalm 25, the great Psalm writer, David, prays for guidance and deliverance. Read the entire Psalm, especially noting verses 8 through 12: "Good and upright is the Lord; therefore He instructs sinners in the way. He leads the humble in what is right, and teaches the humble His way. All the paths of the Lord are steadfast love and faithfulness for those who keep His covenant and His decrees. For Your name's sake, O Lord, pardon my guilt, for it is great. Who are they that fear the Lord? He will teach them the way that they should choose."

In the New Testament, in the teachings of Jesus, we find a great deal of moral instruction. Turn to the Book of Matthew and read The Beatitudes (Matthew 5:1-12) to learn of one of the ways Jesus taught about the sacredness of human life. There is one passage in this book of the Bible that you probably already know: "In everything do to others as you would have them do to you; for this is the law and the prophets." (Matthew 7:12) That is known as the Golden Rule, one of the basics of moral instruction. Continue in the Book of Matthew until you find chapter 22:39. Jesus has just explained that you must love God with all your heart, soul and mind; then he explains that the second most important law we need to remember is "You shall love your neighbor as yourself."

Look through the Bible to see if you can locate other passages that teach about the sacredness of human life. You may want to ask parents, teachers or leaders for Scripture that has helped them to live a moral life. Morality is centered on belief on His commandments and on the guidelines found in the Bible — the Word of God.

In school, when a new subject or idea is presented, we have to learn new vocabulary. Look up the following words so the definitions are clear to you: Kill, moral, morality, guidance, sacred, commandment, destroy and respect. If you have a large dictionary or a thesaurus, a special type of word book, try to find the opposite meaning of each word listed.

Fold a sheet of paper in half lengthwise. List the vocabulary words down the lefthand side of the paper allowing a few lines between words. What do you think the word means? Look up the definitions and record the information; then write the opposing meaning on the other side of the fold.

Read Psalm 25 and the passages from the Book of Matthew mentioned above. Which of those instructions can you memorize?

INDIVIDUAL

Materials

- ❑ Board for checker game
- ❑ Checkers
- ❑ Pencils or pens
- ❑ Bible
- ❑ Index cards, 3" x 5"

Method

The Sixth Commandment states that no one should kill another person. Most of us would never be able to end a human life, but many times we are guilty of taking "life" away from someone by showing disrespect, arguing, criticizing, ignoring or ridiculing. We can "kill" the spirit of a friend or family member with cruel words and thoughts as well as harmful actions.

Jesus has a great deal to say about how each individual must conduct his or her life. Many of Jesus' teachings appear in the writings called the Sermon on the Mount (Matthew 5,6,7,). In Matthew 5:21-24, Jesus reminded listeners that "You shall not murder," but he also warned against being angry without reconciliation or forgiveness. Holding in anger and not forgiving each other are behaviors that can destroy people or groups on either side of the conflict.

God wants us to find healthy and constructive ways to handle our differences so no one is "killed." Remember that we are His most precious creation. We should not only avoid destroying other persons, but we should attempt to move beyond hurtful actions, as well. Think of how you can lend a helping hand to a busy person or bring joy to someone who is lonely. What else can you as an individual do to improve the quality of life of just one other person?

Assemble the parts of this game to play alone or with a friend. This will serve as a reminder that you may make right choices about how you treat others and about following God's commandments.

Read the Bible passage before beginning to make the game. Think about what an individual does that causes pain to another human: put-downs, gossip, rudeness, and so forth. Write one situation for each of ten cards such as: Laugh at new girl because she has funny looking clothes; Do not allow John to play with you because he has an accent; Tease someone until he or she cries. When you have ten (or more if you will be playing with others) cards written, think of positive or life-enhancing circumstances: Include a not-so-popular child to come sit with you and your friends at lunch; Help someone pick up dropped books instead of embarrassing them by laughing; Offer to run errands or do simple chores for an elderly neighbor. Write a card for each of the positive ideas you have.

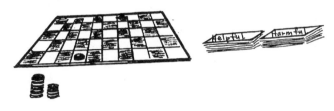

Shuffle the "Harmful" and "Helpful" cards so they are mixed up and face down. Place the checkerboard and checkers in front of you; one checker will be used as a marker, the others will be for payments. Before you begin, write "Harmful" on one blank card and "Helpful" on another. Position the marker on one of the squares at the bottom of the board. Draw the first card and read what it says. If it is a helpful scenario, move your marker up one square; if it is harmful, move it back (the first one may have to move off the board). Continue drawing cards and moving the marker until you reach the top of the row. Every time you go forward, reward yourself by putting one checker on the card that says helpful; when you go back, put one on the card marked harmful.

Follow this plan at least three times, then look at your piles to see which has the most checkers. This type of solitaire will be interesting to see what the results are, but it will be even more fun with one or two other players. Each person will move up one of the rows and keep their own piles of checkers. The person that wins is the one with the most checkers on the helpful pile. In fact, everyone wins when you learn that each individual can make correct choices in honoring all living things and loving all of God's creatures.

ISSUES

Materials

❑ Paper ❑ Pens
❑ Envelopes ❑ Stamps
❑ Felt, fabric or paper ❑ Fabric, felt and paper scraps
❑ Scissors ❑ Glue
❑ Dowel rods ❑ Permanent markers

Advance Preparation

❑ Obtain the names and addresses of organizations that support life such as Save the Whales, Hunger relief agencies, and so forth.

Method

Throughout the United States, and around the world, organizations are responding to the words of the Sixth Commandment, "You shall not kill," in a variety of ways. Groups and individuals advocate for many causes involving issues of abortion, capitol punishment, war, hunger, suicide, euthanasia, infanticide, homicide, murder and more.

Learn about the activities of organizations that promote life as a sacred gift from God. Using the names and addresses provided, write for information on the group's policies, programs, and publications. Address envelopes; stamp and mail the letters.

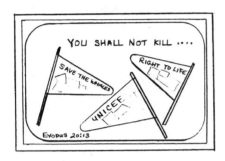

Bulletin Board

When the materials arrive, make flag shaped banners to tell the stories of the groups that were researched. By displaying the information in this way, everyone can learn about the diversity and direction of various organizations. Felt, fabric, or paper may be used for the background of the flags. Cut the material into the shape of a flag or pennant. Using permanent markers, write the name and draw the symbol of the group represented by the flag. As an alternative, this information may be cut from the literature and glued in place. Design and decorate the flags with words and pictures that describe the activities of the agency studied. Tape or glue a dowel rod to one side of the banner.

Banner / Flag

To make the activity even more personal, choose a shape and design that shows a special way in which you support God's gift of life.

Display the completed flags on a bulletin board, or use them in a parade or procession.

CHAPTER EIGHT

The Seventh Commandment

"You shall not commit adultery," the seventh law of God located in the Bible in Exodus 20:14 and Deuteronomy 5:18, is generally associated with keeping the covenant of marriage. Although this is an intended interpretation of the commandment, in a broader sense this theme of faithfulness extends to all aspects of life. Commandment number seven also illustrates that in keeping our covenants, or promises, we are reminded of the faithfulness of God to His people — God keeps His covenants with us.

Learn more about the interpretation of the seventh commandment by using the activities for five learning centers. "Commandments" invites exploration of significance and symbol; "Characteristics" indicates actions and attitudes necessary for a covenant keeper; "Commitment" imparts information on treating our bodies as the temple of the Holy Spirit; and "Choices" individualizes responsibility for keeping God's guidelines. All of the activities, individually and collectively, serve to remind the participants that God's laws are a guide to love by in all areas of their lives.

COMMANDMENTS

Materials

- Bible
- Scissors
- String
- Yardstick
- Ballpoint pens
- Glue sticks
- Hole punch
- Florist's or giftwrap ribbon, 1" wide; assorted colors
- Construction paper (9" x 12") in bright colors

Method

God has created a well-ordered world! The Ten Commandments, as well as all the other laws in the Bible, are guides to help us live the kind of life God intends. Review the commandments you know already, add this new law, "You shall not commit adultery," then look ahead to the remainder of the list. Read the Commandments in Exodus 20:1-17 or Deuteronomy 5:1-22, mark the place, and set the Bible aside for now.

Create a decorative, woven windsock to help you remember each of the commandments. Hang it where you can easily review the list! Select the paper and ribbon colors you like for the windsock. Fold the construction paper in half lengthwise and cut along the fold to form two 4 1/2"

Fold then
cut along fold

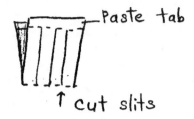

Paste tab

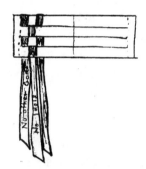

↑ cut slits

by 12" strips. Place one of the strips in front of you, fold it in half the short way, then fold up the two ends ... about 1/2 inch ... to form paste tabs. Cut three parallel slits in the folded paper, starting at the fold in the middle and stopping at the creased tabs at the end. Carefully unfold the paper and place it flat on the work surface. Cut ten ribbons about 18 inches long. Open the Bible to the Ten Commandments and print them in order, one per ribbon. A ballpoint pen will work best on the shiny ribbon. If the commandment is too long to fit, abbreviate it or just include the key words. Weave the first ribbon into the paper slits by going under, over, under and over. Scoot the ribbon as near to the folded end as possible; then fasten it with glue at the top. Weave the second ribbon over, under, over and under. Continue with this alternating pattern until all ten ribbons are woven into the paper "loom" and all are secured. Glue the remaining piece of paper to the back of the woven strip to strengthen the weaving.

Finish the project by forming the woven piece into a cylinder and by gluing the overlapped paste tabs. Punch three holes, evenly spaced, near the top edge and fasten strings. Tie the three pieces of string together to form a hanger.

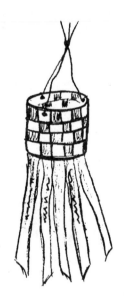

Enjoy the movement of the windsock, memorize the commandments and think about the ways God's laws are "woven" into your life!

COVENANT

Materials

- ❏ Bible
- ❏ Embroidery floss
- ❏ Beading needles
- ❏ Tape
- ❏ Instructions for various friendship bracelets or knotting techniques
- ❏ Hymnal or Book of Worship
- ❏ Beads
- ❏ Scissors
- ❏ Thread, fine
- ❏ Charms, small (rainbow, star, heart)

Method

Throughout the Bible, there are descriptions of covenants between God and a person or a group. On occasion, there are accounts of covenants between individuals. What is a covenant? Sometimes a covenant is defined as a "binding agreement or a solemn promise between two people or groups." Other words associated with covenant are ... pledge, vow, faithful, fidelity, loyalty, honor, pact, and commitment.

Two familiar covenant stories are found in the Book of Genesis. Learn about God's promise to Noah in Genesis 8:20-22 and 9:1-17. What is the symbol associated with God's promise? (Genesis 9:12-17) Another covenant story (Genesis 15:1-6) concerns Abram and God. What depicts this pledge? (Genesis 15:5) The Seventh Commandment deals with an important part of God's plan for the future of His people — faithfulness. This law, telling us not to commit adultery, is God's plan for protecting marriage and the family where children can grow and learn in loving surroundings. The commandment requires that husbands and wives honor the vows made on their wedding day.

You may have been to a wedding and felt the happiness and love of this special covenant ceremony. The couple promises to each other, to God, and to all of the friends and relatives that they will be faithful and will always love the other person. In some churches, the people gathered pledge to help the couple honor their wedding vows! Keeping promises is sometimes very hard to do. God does not expect us to be perfect; He forgives us when we fail, but He does insist on us trying our best. We may need to renew our vows of love and faithfulness—everyday—and we may have to ask for God's help to keep our promises—everyday.

Look in your church's hymnal or book of worship for the Service of Christian Marriage or the Service of Holy Matrimony. The terms may vary in different churches, but see if you can find the words — covenant, vow, pledge or promise. The wedding band is a special part of the marriage covenant, because a ring has been universally accepted as a symbol of eternal union.

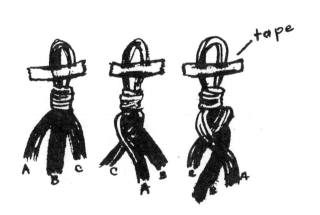

Did you ever tie a string around your finger as a reminder to do something? In this activity, you will design a "reminder ring" to help you remember to keep promises. There are several Methods to create a unique ring. A simple plan is to cut twelve or fifteen strands of embroidery floss about six inches long. Knot all of the pieces on one end and tape securely to the table. Divide the floss into three bunches and braid until you have a little more than an inch remaining. Form a knot near the braided portion and remove the tape from the other knotted end. Get help to tie this simple ring around your finger. Trim off excess floss if the finished piece is too long.

You may already know some special knotting techniques that are used to fashion friendship bracelets. Craft stores and libraries have "how-to" books with step by step diagrams. Try one of those methods to form a "reminder ring."

Make the ring more attractive by adding beads as each knot is formed. Choose beads that will slide easily onto the floss and ones that will be smooth next to your skin. If you can find a craft or bead shop with small charms, look for a rainbow, star or heart to remind you of particular covenants. Fasten the charms to the knots with a needle and fine thread. Be sure to stitch over and over to hold the charm securely in place. You may want to make several rings to share with friends. When you wear the ring, remember God expects us to keep promises and to be faithful.

CHARACTERISTICS

Materials

- ❑ Dictionary
- ❑ Bible dictionary or concordance
- ❑ Pens
- ❑ Scissors
- ❑ Container such as a margarine tub
- ❑ Bible
- ❑ Paper
- ❑ Magazines
- ❑ Glue

Method

Here is an important question: What is a covenant? Look up the word in a dictionary and remember that a covenant is an agreement or promise. Also look up the word in a Bible dictionary or concordance and see what Scripture has to say about this topic.

An even more important question to consider is: What kind of person keeps a promise? Or, another way to put it is: What are the characteristics of a covenant, or commandment, keeper? Characteristics are distinguishing traits or qualities. Take a piece of paper and a pen and make a list of five to ten traits of someone who keeps promises. There are no right and wrong answers; just list the first thoughts that come to mind. Words might include courageous, strong, loyal, trustworthy, committed, dependable, problem solver, honest, responsible, truthful, dedicated, earnest, devoted, brave, and bold.

Use these and other words to write a unique poem, called a Dada, about the characteristics of a covenant keeper. Dada, a very easy form of poetry to write, was originally invented by artists and poets in Paris, France who clipped words from newspapers, scrambled them, and then arranged them in lines to form thoughts and themes. Select ten or more words to use for the project, and write them on small pieces of paper or cut them from printed material, such as old magazines. After writing or finding the words place them in a container, mix them up, and draw them out one at a time. Arrange the words on a piece of paper until they express the desired thought. Experiment with various ways in which the words can be combined. Tape or glue them in place. Illustrations may be added.

COMMITMENT

Materials

- ❑ Bulletin board
- ❑ Scrap paper for patterns
- ❑ Markers
- ❑ Fabric pieces
- ❑ Yardstick
- ❑ Tape
- ❑ Pre-cut letters or letter patterns
- ❑ Glue sticks or white glue
- ❑ Construction paper, assorted colors
- ❑ Pencils
- ❑ Scissors
- ❑ Hair-colored yarn
- ❑ Thumbtacks
- ❑ Small paper plates
- ❑ Stapler and staples

Advance Preparation

☐ Cover the bulletin board with red or another bold color.

☐ Add the caption "Fearfully and Wonderfully Made" with purchased or cut out letters.

Method

God created human bodies with all kinds of feelings of pain and pleasure but the most important truth to understand is that our body is a temple for the Holy Spirit. In the Seventh Commandment, God instructs us to be faithful in body, mind and soul. When we make a commitment or pledge to follow God's way, we are expected to be faithful to the commandments. Similarly, when we marry, we will make a commitment to our partner to be faithful in body, mind and soul. "You shall not commit adultery" is the law that reminds married people of their special covenant relationship. As well, unmarried people must be faithful to the commitments they make.

God expects all of us to take good care of the body we have and to show respect for ourselves as well as others. Read Psalm 139 to discover what the Psalmist, David, had to say about our "design." Verse 14 praises God: "I praise you, for I am fearfully and wonderfully made. Wonderful are your works; that I know very well." We can show praise and express appreciation to God for the way He created us, by making a commitment to use our bodies and minds with the best possible intentions, not for immoral purposes.

Assemble a simple figure of yourself to display on a bulletin board featuring the theme "Fearfully and wonderfully made." Choose paper suitable for skin tones, then form a basic figure of a person using large geometric shapes. For the head, trace a small paper plate; for the torso, one 9" x 12" sheet of paper; for the legs and arms, two 9" x 12" pieces of paper, cut in half lengthwise. Trim the "arm" strips so they are not too long. Add triangles for hands and feet or draw your own. Assemble the body parts by using tape or glue on the back of the sections.

"Dress" the figure by using the body as a pattern to trace a shirt and jeans or a shirt on fabric. Cut the shirt and jeans to fit the arms, legs and torso. If the figure is going to be wearing a skirt, shape the fabric so it flares out or cut it much wider, then pleat with staples or glue. Glue on yarn strands to form curly or straight hair. Cut out a red heart and glue it to the shirt. Finish the person by adding facial features with markers.

Cut strips of paper to make labels for parts of the body:

- **head** — to learn about God's laws;

- **eyes** — to see the wonders God has created;

- **ears** — to hear the stories from the Bible;

- **mouth** — to sing praises to God;

- **heart** — to feel and share God's love;

- **hands** — to help others;

- **feet** — to be a messenger to spread the Gospel.

Can you think of special gifts or talents you have that can be added to these labels?

Tack the figure to a bulletin board at home or add it to a group display in the classroom. As you view the display, remember that your body is a temple for the Holy Spirit. Ask God for guidance and courage to honor your commitment to remain faithful in body, mind and soul!

CHOICES

Materials

- ❑ Bible
- ❑ Rulers
- ❑ Bowl for buttons
- ❑ Pens
- ❑ Markers
- ❑ Buttons
- ❑ Index cards
- ❑ Cardboard shirt box tops and bottoms

Advance Preparation

- ❑ Number index cards 1-9. Write a Scripture passage or a life situation involving keeping or breaking promises on each card. Suggestions for "life situation" questions include:

  - Tyler promises to keep the secret Ashley told him, but Jacob asks Tyler what Ashley said. Should he tell?

  - Harrison agrees to be home by 10:00 P.M., but his friends invite him to a movie that starts at 9:45 P.M. Should he go?

  - Kyla tells her brother that she'll walk the dog, but she'd rather watch her favorite television show. What should she do?

Ideas for Scripture passages to look up and read are:
- Genesis 9:15,16 — God's covenant with Noah

- Genesis 17:7 — God's covenant with Abraham

- Exodus 24:3-8 — The Ten Commandments

The Seventh Commandment is about promises, also called vows, commitments, covenants, agreements, and many other words. Once a person makes a promise he or she has a choice: to keep the commitment or to break it. Sometimes people think it's ok to break a covenant because "everybody else is doing it," but that isn't true! Play a game about "choices" and learn more about keeping promises.

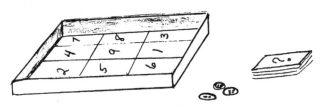

Make a gameboard. Select the top or the bottom of a flat cardboard box. With a ruler and crayon or marker, draw two horizontal lines and two vertical lines across the inside of the box. This will make nine oblong spaces. Number the spaces one through nine, mixing up the numbers. Use a button as the playing piece. Hold the button at least twelve inches above the box, close your eyes, and drop the button into the gameboard. If it falls on a line, take another turn. Select the question that corresponds with the number on the square where the button landed. Try to answer the question or look up the Scripture passage and read it. Take at least three turns. Write additional questions on index cards for others to try.

The Eighth Commandment

In the Eighth Commandment God tells His people: "You shall not steal." This Law forbids taking something that another person or group truly owns and intends to keep, or more simply stated, it means taking something away from someone to whom it belongs. People steal from self, others, and God. They steal possessions, money, talents, time, and more. There are many types of stealing: robbery, shoplifting, kidnapping, fraud, abuse; the list goes on and on.

It is interesting to note that Jesus does not directly mention the Eighth Commandment in the New Testament, rather he refers to meeting human need and emphasizes that justice takes place when those who "have" help those who "have not."

Five Learning Center activities are designed to help participants explore various aspects of the Eighth Commandment and to apply the information and insights to their own lives. "Practice" involves a review of the Law of God; "Purpose" introduces the intent of the Eighth Commandment; "Positive" includes references on Jesus' teaching regarding stealing; "Possessions" identifies ways to rightfully obtain items; and "Protection" illustrates that true security comes from trust in God. Use the experiences to learn more about another of God's "Laws to love by."

PRACTICE

Materials

- ❏ Bible
- ❏ Paper
- ❏ Copy machine
- ❏ Ten Commandment Action Story
- ❏ Pens or pencils

Advance Preparation

- ❏ Duplicate a copy of the "Action Story" for each participant.

Method

Exodus 20:1-21 and Deuteronomy 5:1-22 record God's teachings known as the Ten Commandments. Review these guides for living by using the action story provided and by writing one of your own.

Read the story, silently or out loud, and make the suggested gestures at the appropriate time. Find another student and try the story together. Read the Commandments in Exodus or

Deuteronomy and write your own action story. Paper and pens or pencils are provided for this purpose. Take copies with you and teach either or both stories to someone else!

TEN COMMANDMENTS ACTION STORY[1]

Commandment number one
Is simple to recall:
There is only one God
Jehovah, Lord of all.
[Raise one finger.]

Commandment number two
Has good advice for you.
Do not serve any idols
There's just one God that's true.
[Raise two fingers.]

God's name is very special
Hold it in high regard.
That's commandment number three.
That isn't very hard.
[Raise three fingers.]

Sunday is a special day
Do not work, but rest.
The fourth commandment tells us
That Sunday is the best.
[Raise four fingers.]

Your father and your mother
Are gifts from God to you.
Commandment number five says
Honor them in all you do.
[Raise five fingers.]

Do not murder is number six,
The commandment after five.
The special creatures God has made
Must all be kept alive.
[Raise six fingers.]

Be faithful to the one you love
Is seven's guide for life.
This is a good commandment
For a husband and a wife.
[Raise seven fingers.]

Commandment eight says do not take
What does not belong to you.
By keeping this commandment
You praise God in all you do.
[Raise eight fingers.]

Don't bear false witness, number nine
Means in everything you do
You must tell the truth about others
It is God's law for you.
[Raise nine fingers.]

There may be things that others have
That you'd like to have too.
Number ten says do not covet.
This is God's guide for you.
[Raise ten fingers.]

[1]Wezeman, Phyllis Vos. Fifty-Two Bible Stories In Rhyme And Rhythm, (Carthage, IL: Shining Star), 1995. Used by permission.

PURPOSE

Materials

- Bibles
- Heavy drawing paper
- Brushes
- Containers
- Candle stubs or paraffin
- Construction paper
- Black, blue or violet watercolors or tempera paints
- Pencils
- Scissors
- Water
- Crayons
- Newspaper
- Ruler

Method

The Eighth Commandment is probably one of the first commandments you learned ... right along with your parents' instructions to share and to play peacefully! As a very young child you began to understand that it is wrong to take something that does not belong to you.

When Moses received the Laws from God, Israel was a very young nation. The people of God traveled and lived together for many years. It was necessary to have definite guidelines in order for them to live peacefully. Respecting the property and possessions of each person was very important in those times, just as it is today. God commands us to avoid stealing and cheating and He expects us to respect the belongings of others. Being trustworthy makes it easier to live in harmony with our friends and neighbors. It is very normal to want what someone else has, but stealing is not an acceptable way to get things. God wants us to eliminate any behavior that stands in the way of fulfilling our covenant with Him.

Look up Matthew 6:9-13 and read The Lord's Prayer, which Jesus taught the disciples. In many versions of the Bible, the words are: "Lead us not into temptation," and in others it is written: "And do not bring us to the time of trial," with a foot-note explaining that the phrase means "temptation." In order to keep the Eighth Commandment, we must resist temptation!

It will be helpful to look up The Lord's Prayer as well as The Ten Commandments. (Exodus 20:1-17 or Deuteronomy 5:1-22) Design a sign or poster which will be a reminder to keep God's laws. Just for fun, since we are thinking about "resisting," try the art method known as "crayon resist." In this process, an image or design is colored with a waxy crayon and a wash of diluted paint is brushed over the surface. The painted color will adhere to the paper, but the waxy areas will resist the diluted paint.

Read the Scripture passages from Exodus, Deuteronomy and Matthew in different versions of the Bible and select one for your sign: "Do not steal," "Thou shalt not steal," "You shall not steal," "Neither shall you steal;" or you may choose, "Lead us not into temptation."

On a piece of light-colored drawing paper, create bubble or block letters. Design the words with bold patterns, like polka dots or stripes, and fill in with bright colors. Press heavily with crayons as you decorate the letters. If the crayons are not very waxy, it may be helpful to rub over the colored areas with a candle stub or a chunk of paraffin.

Cover the work space with newspapers, put paint in a small container, then add water to prepare the wash. Try out the paint to see if there is enough intensity without being opaque. Add more water or paint as needed. Brush paint from one side of the paper to the other, repeating strokes until the entire sign is covered. The wash should form "beads" or bubbles on the colored words creating a contrast between the dark painted areas and the waxy surfaces. Set the sign aside and allow it to dry. You may choose to make a construction paper frame to give the artwork a more finished look. Each time you look at the words, remember that God wants us to resist temptation.

POSITIVE

Materials

- ❑ Construction paper
- ❑ Pencils
- ❑ Yarn
- ❑ Heart patterns
- ❑ Concordance or Bible dictionary
- ❑ Scratch paper
- ❑ Scissors
- ❑ Tape
- ❑ Hole punch
- ❑ Bible
- ❑ Markers

Method

There are many rules guiding us in our relationship with God and with each other. The Ten Commandments summarize the basic laws and instruct us in our covenant with God. In his New Covenant, Jesus tells us in a positive way how to live. Instead of "You-shall-not," he emphasizes "You-shall." When asked which commandment was the greatest, Jesus set forth the Law in two important commandments of love for God and love for neighbor. (Matthew 22:36-40) You shall love the Lord your God with all your heart, and with all your soul, and with all your mind. This is the greatest and first commandment. And a second is like it: You shall love your neighbor as yourself."

When you truly love your neighbor, you will not commit an act against that person, such as: killing, unfaithfulness, stealing, lying or coveting. In fact, Jesus directs us to give to others and teaches His followers to go into action for justice. We know that it is wrong to take something that is not ours; we learn from Jesus, that not sharing when someone is in need is equally wrong.

Can you think of ways to meet needs of people who might benefit from your help?

Look up the word "neighbor" in a concordance or Bible dictionary, especially the New Testament references. The main theme in those scripture passages is LOVE! Fashion a mobile of hearts to symbolize the covenant we have with our Creator and with our fellow human beings. Read the "neighbor" passages before you begin this activity in order to understand how Jesus expects us to love others. Make some notes about verses you like.

Select red paper or a variety of colors for the hearts, then trace and cut out hearts of several sizes. On the largest heart, print Matthew 22:36-40 and on the flip side, print Exodus 20:1- 17. You may choose to write out the entire verse or just key words. On the smaller hearts, indicate

some of the other verses you have read or write out words such as: love, neighbor, share, justice, covenant.

Assemble a "one-string" mobile by placing the yarn vertically in front of you and taping the smaller hearts one after the other in one long line. Tape the yarn to the back of each heart. Place the largest heart at the top and tape it to the string of hearts. Punch a hole in the center at the top of the large heart. Tie on a short loop of yarn for hanging. As your heart mobile swings in the breeze, think of ways to show love to your neighbor!

POSSESSIONS

Materials

- ❑ Scissors
- ❑ Art tissue in assorted colors
- ❑ Brushes
- ❑ Pencils
- ❑ Gel medium or decoupage materials
- ❑ Knife
- ❑ Glue sticks
- ❑ Paper
- ❑ Permanent markers
- ❑ Small sturdy boxes with lids or cans with plastic lids

Method

The Eighth Commandment focuses on possessions. All of us own certain things that we have earned money to buy or that we have received as special gifts. We do not expect to have our possessions stolen from us. Everyone feels hurt or disappointed when belongings are taken. God wants us to be able to trust and to be trustworthy.

We need to keep in mind that all of our "things" are on loan from God. We are not supposed to accumulate lots of valuables and selfishly guard them. God does not intend for us to be so concerned about our possessions that we forget about people who have nothing.

In addition to material possessions, each of us has unique talents, personal reputation, and distinct personality. We steal from ourselves, as well as from our Creator, if we do not share our God-given abilities and our lives with others. We steal from another person if we do something to damage a reputation or a "good name."

Children learn at a very early age that any kind of stealing is wrong. It is helpful to learn that we can ask God to guide us when we are tempted and to forgive us if we make a mistake. God gave us the power to think and the ability to make choices. How can you use those gifts to get what you want?

List all of the options you can think of for obtaining something you really want. Ideas include earn, trade, make, buy, borrow, and share. Also list ways to earn money to purchase items that you would like to own. Create an attractive bank to hold any money you save for buying something

gel medium

special. You will decorate the bank with tissue paper collage.

Choose a container for your bank. Use the knife and carefully cut the coin slot in the lid of the can or box. Cut or tear pieces of colorful tissue paper and glue them to the outside of the container. Continue until the entire outer surface is covered.

Follow the directions on the bottle of gel medium. Brush the gloss over the tissue to give it a shiny, durable covering. Allow the medium to dry, then apply another coat, if needed. When the bank is completely dry, use the permanent marker to write on a Scripture reference or to draw symbols. Place your written list near or inside the bank; read it from time to time to remain aware of the many choices there are for getting what you want!

PROTECTION

Materials

- Paper
- Index cards
- Scissors
- Magazines

- Pens or pencils
- Markers
- Glue
- Newspapers

Method

Some people's response to the eighth commandment, "You shall not steal," is to surround themselves with security. Although guarding one's property, possessions, and person is a wise idea, it is important to remember that the real source of the Christian's security is God. Several Psalms illustrate this truth. Psalm 121, subtitled "Assurance of God's Protection," is a wonderful example. Look up the Psalm in the Bible and read the words.

Crime statistics in the United States are staggering. According to the Federal Bureau of Investigation, a division of the U. S. Department of Justice, a violent crime or a property crime is committed in the United States every two seconds. Figures like these have forced people to seek security in numerous ways. Elderly men and women live in locked houses. Business owners guard their property by placing metal bars over windows and iron grates over doors. Drivers lock their car doors and use devices such as "The Club" to deter auto theft. Women who go out alone often carry whistles or alarms to prevent attack. Travelers are inconvenienced by metal detectors and security screening at airports. If people kept the Eighth Commandment would any of this be necessary?

Explore the theme of "protection" and discover ways to empower people to respond with effective actions. Select a piece of paper and a pen or pencil and start a list of evidences of protection that are all around us. Answers might include: barbed wire; fences; metal shutters; "The Club" on steering wheels; bars on windows; metal detectors in public buildings, schools, and airports; security guards; signs and decals indicating protection services and devices. Once the list is developed find illustrations of many of these forms of "protection." This can be done by locating pictures in magazines and newspapers or by drawing the examples. Regardless of the method used to obtain the pictures, two examples of each type of "Protection" are needed so a game of "Concentration" may be played with the illustrations. Use materials such as index cards, magazines, newspapers, scissors and glue and create two identical cards for each example.

Shuffle the papers and lay them out, picture side down, in a tiled pattern on the floor or on a table. Play the game in the following way. Turn two cards over. If they match, another turn may be taken. If they do not match, the cards are returned to a face-down position. Attempt to make another match by turning over two more cards. Play continues until all pairs have been uncovered. Each time a match is made, share one way to address the issue illustrated on the cards. For example, if the picture of a locked car appears, the player might suggest an escort or pick-up service for the elderly. A response to a picture of bars on windows or gates on doors could be to establish a neighborhood crime watch. For the illustration of metal detectors at schools, an educational program on drugs could be offered.

When the game is over, use the pictures as a bulletin board display. Re-read Psalm 121 and remember that the true source of security and protection is God.

CHAPTER TEN

The Ninth Commandment

It sounds so simple: "You shall not bear false witness against your neighbor." [Exodus 20:16] In other words, "Don't lie." Yet, the words of the ninth commandment are very difficult to keep. Every day people bear false witness against individuals and groups. They deceive themselves, their neighbors and their God by blaspheming and boasting, demeaning and distorting, maligning and misrepresenting. Individuals bear false witness for power, pride and profit with words, thoughts, and deeds. And, when people bear false witness they erode the truth and evade reality.

God's law to love by is really very basic. "We are called to speak the truth in any situation in which we have a responsibility to communicate at all." [Smedes, Lewis B. Mere Morality: What God Expects From Ordinary People. Grand Rapids, MI: Eerdmans, 1983] There is an instruction booklet called The Small Catechism by Martin Luther. In the little handbook, each commandment is interpreted after the question, "What does this mean for us?" The "false witness" commandment is explained in a positive way: "We are to fear and love God so that we do not betray, slander, or lie about our neighbor, but defend him or her, speak well of her of him, and explain his actions in the kindest way."

Through exploring and experiencing the activities in five Learning Centers, participants will discover the message and the meaning of the Ninth Commandment. "Teach" deals with a review of the Ten Commandments; "Truth" defines the meaning of false witness; "Types" describes examples of false witness in everyday situations; "Texts" depicts the Law in light of Scripture passages related to the theme; and "Trust" develops an activity involving forgiveness. Use the exercises as part of a continuing study of the Ten Commandments or as a supplement to a lesson on lying.

TEACH

Materials

- ❑ Index cards, ten per participant
- ❑ Bible
- ❑ Markers or pens
- ❑ Bags

Method

Before beginning a study of the Ninth Commandment, review all ten of God's "Laws to Love by." Make pieces for a "Grab Bag" game to use during this activity and to use later as a way to help teach the Ten Commandments to others.

Number ten index cards one through ten. On the back side of each card write that number's commandment. Place the ten cards in a bag. Draw one card at a time out of the bag. If you look at the number side first, recite the commandment. If you look at the commandment side first, give the number. Play the game alone or with another person. For an extra challenge, think about or say one way in which keeping the Commandment helps you show love for God and for others.

TRUTH

Materials

- Scissors
- Ruler
- Pencils
- Glue sticks
- Magazines

- Colored construction paper (9" x 12")
- Self-stick labels for mailing or file folder
- Markers
- Paper scraps

Method

"Do not bear false witness against your neighbor," instructs the Ninth Commandment. In some versions of the Bible, the words say, "Do not lie," or "Do not give false testimony against your neighbor." God expects us to be truthful. Truth means that which is true, exact, honest and sincere.

To tell the good things about a person might be helpful, to gossip about someone's bad actions may be hurtful; but to say a person has done something bad which he or she has NOT really done is "bearing false witness" and can cause much harm. Falsely blaming or accusing another person and not taking responsibility for one's own actions is what this commandment is all about.

When we are untruthful about a neighbor or tell the neighbor a lie, we deceive ourselves as well as the other person. God is offended when we lie to others and when we try to fool ourselves into believing what is untrue. God knows if we are being honest! The Ninth Commandment reminds us that God plans for us to be truthful, dependable and faithful to Him, to ourselves and to our family, friends and everyone else.

Speaking the truth is just one way to follow the commandment; we must also consider thoughts and actions. Thinking untrue thoughts about someone can be harmful to us and to the other person, for it may affect our feelings toward him or her. Actions may speak louder falsehoods than words. For instance, you see your best friend take another person's lunch money and you walk the other way as if you saw nothing. Can you think of other examples that show ways people "bear false witness" in words, thoughts and actions? What can be done to "un-do" the wrong?

Create a "mini-kiosk" prayer prompter to be displayed on a shelf or desk top. Kiosks are free-standing bulletin boards that are usually covered with posters and advertising slogans. Place one piece of colored paper horizontally in front of you on the table. Fold the paper into three sections, approximately 3 and 1/2 inches across, which will allow for a 1 and 1/2 inch paste tab along the side. Write one phrase per label: True to God, True to Self, True to Other —or—Truthful Words, Truthful Actions, Truthful Thoughts. Stick one label on each section of the kiosk. You may want to use the second set of labels on the reverse side of the folded paper. Apply a small bit of

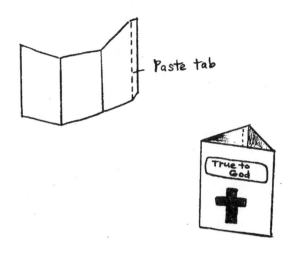

Paste tab

glue to the paste tab and form the kiosk into a triangular, free-standing column. Add personal touches with symbols cut from paper or appropriate pictures cut from magazines. For example, if you are using "God, others, self" you might create symbols or cut out pictures such as a cross, groups of people, and objects that relate to you and your interests. Arrange the collage and glue the pieces to the column. You may want to add a favorite scripture passage. Place your prayer prompter where you can see it and use it as a reminder to ask for God's help to be truthful always in words, actions and thoughts to God, self and others.

TYPES

Materials

- ❑ "False Witness" Game
- ❑ Copier
- ❑ Dictionary
- ❑ Paper
- ❑ Pencils or pens

Method

When we hear or read the words of the Ninth Commandment, "You shall not bear false witness," our minds conjure up a picture of a witness in a court room testifying that he is about to speak the truth, the whole truth, and nothing but the truth, so help him God. But the Commandment applies to a whole range of human activities in which the truth is set over against the lie. There are many types of bearing false witness that people encounter or engage in every day. Play a matching game to learn more about this theme.

The list in the left column are words that name nine different types of bearing false witness. Look up each term in the dictionary and make notes on the definitions. The statements in the right column are everyday examples of ways in which people bear false witness against one another. Choose the word on the left that best describes the statement on the right and draw a line to connect the two.

FALSE WITNESS GAME

LEFT COLUMN	RIGHT COLUMN
1. Backbiting	A. Nardis makes up statistics for a book report.
2. Boasting	B. Kareemah tells Glenn that his science project was not as good as the judges said it was.

3. Demeaning	C. Jennifer and Shelley tell Melissa they really like her dress, and after she leaves they talk about how awful it looks.
4. Exaggeration	D. Dakota tells all his friends that Kara cheated on the test when she didn't.
5. Fraud	E. Cindy claims that Peter's accident was not a big deal.
6. Glosses	F. For many years the United States government claimed that the people of the Soviet Union were bad.
7. Propaganda	G. Nathan talks about all the trophies he has received in track.
8. Rumor	H. Kelly does not stand up to her friends when they make racial slurs against other students.
9. Silence	I. Craig tells D.J. that the fish he caught was two feet when it was only seven inches.

ANSWERS

1 - C; 2 - G; 3 - B; 4 - I; 5 - A; 6 - E; 7 - F; 8 - D; 9 - H.

TEXTS

Materials

- ❑ Bible
- ❑ Clear tape
- ❑ Scissors
- ❑ Ruler
- ❑ Markers
- ❑ Ribbon or yarn
- ❑ Paper, white or light-colored, 3" x 18"
- ❑ Paper strips for bookmarks
- ❑ Cardboard squares, 3-1/2 inches (2 per book)
- ❑ Glue sticks
- ❑ Wallpaper or gift wrap
- ❑ Hole punch
- ❑ Pencils

Method

God wants us always to be truthful! The Bible ... our own handbook for "right living" ... is filled with informative and inspirational scripture intended to guide us. There are numerous passages concerned with being truthful and trustworthy. Locate and read the following Bible verses: Exodus 20:16; Proverbs 13:5; Psalm 34:11-14; Proverbs 19:5,9; Psalm 15; Ephesians 4:14- 15; Proverbs 6:16-19; John 14:6; Proverbs 12:22. Place a bookmark at the listed scripture readings so you can refer to them again. Choose one of the scripture passages for this activity. You will learn how to make a simple book in the Japanese style of bookbinding.

Fan fold the 3 inch by 18 inch strip, forming 3 inch squares. Crease carefully so all of the sections are uniform. Open up the accordion folded strip to allow for writing the story or scripture. You may choose to put a few words or a phrase in each section. Add any drawings or symbols you can think of to help illustrate the main idea. Perhaps you would like to explore the Book of Proverbs to find additional verses about truth ... one for each page of your book. Set the folded

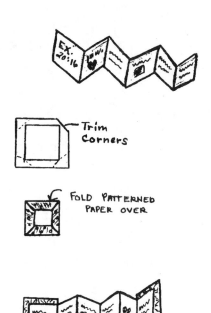

Trim Corners

Fold Patterned Paper Over

pages aside as you make the two cover pieces. Select patterned giftwrap or wallpaper and measure two squares a little larger than the 3 inch cardboard squares. Center the cardboard piece over the patterned paper; then trim off the corners of the larger paper. Fold the flaps over the cardboard and tape in place. Repeat the process with the second piece of cardboard. Place the folded strip in front of you, in position to be read. Spread a little glue over the taped area and attach the first end of the folded strip to form the front cover; glue the back cover to the last section of the strip. Cut ribbon or yarn long enough to tie around the book to keep it closed when it is not being read. Another way to fasten the book is to punch a small hole on the front and back book covers, tie on pieces of ribbon or yarn, then tie the two ends together to form a bow at the edge of a Japanese style book.

Display the special book on your bookshelf or desk as a reminder of the Ninth Commandment. Maybe you would like to make other books as gifts!

TRUST

Materials

- ❏ Paper or styrofoam cups
- ❏ Scissors
- ❏ Glue
- ❏ Tape
- ❏ Pencils
- ❏ Yarn
- ❏ Paper or felt scraps
- ❏ Markers
- ❏ Fabric or tissue paper
- ❏ Bibles

Method

The Ninth Commandment instructs us to be trustworthy, in other words, reliable and dependable. When you say "No" you mean "No," and when you say "Yes," you mean "Yes." In order to get along in civilized communities, we need to trust and to be trusted. If people are always honest, it is easy to put your trust in them.

There is a great deal of information in the Bible about how we are supposed to live so that others believe us and trust us; but how are we expected to respond when someone "bears false witness" against us? What if a classmate tells a lie about you that makes you look bad or gets you in trouble?

Just as God forgives us and loves us when we "goof up," we need to forgive others when they make mistakes. Jesus taught his disciples a prayer that we know as The Lord's Prayer. (Matthew 6:9-13) If you do not already know the prayer, read it and try to memorize it. Directly following The Lord's Prayer is a passage on forgiving: "For if you forgive others their trespasses, your heavenly Father will also forgive you; but if you do not forgive others neither will your Father forgive your trespasses." (Matthew 6:14-15)

Think of several situations that depict telling the truth, earning trust, "bearing false witness," defending someone or showing forgiveness. Make simple cup puppets to dramatize the event or predicament.

HOLE for "NOSE"

Select a cup to use for the project. Using a pencil or scissor points, poke a hole in the side of the cup for the nose. Be sure the opening is about 2 inches up from the cup's rim and that it is large enough for your index finger. Create interesting characters by gluing on scraps of paper, felt or yarn for hair and features. Add details with markers.

Make a "wagging tongue" puppet by poking the hole nearer the rim of the cup, then glue a nose above it. You may wish to design one puppet that "blabs" or "bears false witness" and one that is forgiving. In order to make a simple garment, snip a small hole in the center of a square of fabric or tissue paper. Place your index finger through the garment hole, then into the cup hole. Cut holes for thumb and pinky finger to see the puppet's "arms."

Use your imagination to dramatize possible situations. Practice by yourself and make plans to share the puppet shows with another person or group.

CHAPTER ELEVEN

The Tenth Commandment

"You shall not covet," the words of the Tenth Commandment, found in Exodus 20:17 and Deuteronomy 5:21 should be easy to keep. People should not desire what other people have. They should not even let thoughts about wanting what rightfully belongs to another enter their heads, or their hearts. "You shall not covet" attacks the thought behind the deed and suggests that wrong ideas precede wrong actions.

Some commentators say that covetousness, the topic of the Tenth Commandment, is the beginning of breaking the other nine, for if people do not "covet," they will be less likely to steal, kill, commit adultery, or put other gods before their Creator, Jehovah. And yet, it almost seems like this Commandment is asking the impossible. Humans on their own strength cannot obey this rule. It becomes obvious that they must seek strength from beyond themselves — from a loving, forgiving, purposeful God.

In order to help participants understand the significance of God's tenth "law to love by," use the activities in the five learning centers in Sunday classes, as well as mid-week activities. "Guidelines" surveys the Ten Commandments; "Greed" submits a definition of covetousness; "Goal" stresses blessings rather than desires; "Gospel" studies Jesus' teachings on the subject; and "Generosity" suggests giving rather than getting. All five activities emphasize that the Tenth Commandment offers guidance for loving God and others.

GUIDELINES

Materials

- ❏ Paper
- ❏ Pencils
- ❏ Duplicating equipment
- ❏ Bibles

Method

Although the Ten Commandments were recorded by Moses in the Old Testament books of Exodus and Deuteronomy, each of God's laws were summarized by Jesus in various passages in the New Testament Gospels. It is necessary to know God's laws, but it is also important to understand Jesus's interpretation and intent so that they can be used as guides for our lives.

Play a game that involves looking up a variety of New Testament Scripture passages and matching each of them with one of the Ten Commandments recorded in the Old Testament. Draw lines to connect the right answers. It might be helpful to write a few words that summarize the

New Testament teaching next to the Scripture reference.

THE TEN COMMANDMENTS: OLD & NEW

<u>OLD TESTAMENT</u>   <u>NEW TESTAMENT</u>

1. You shall have no other gods before me.   A. Matthew 19:18

2. You shall not make any graven images.   B. Matthew 12:8; Mark 2:27, 28; Mark 3:4

3. You shall not take the name of the Lord your God in vain. C. Matthew 5:28,29

4. Remember the sabbath day to keep it holy.   D. Luke 12:13-15

5. Honor your father and your mother.   E. Mark 12:30

6. You shall not kill.   F. Matthew 5:34,35

7. You shall not commit adultery.   G. Matthew 6:12

8. You shall not steal.   H. Matthew 6:33; John 4:24

9. You shall not bear false witness against your neighbor. I. Matthew 5:21,22

10. You shall not covet.   J. Matthew 15:4-9

ANSWERS

1. E; 2. H; 3. F; 4. B; 5. J; 6. I; 7. C; 8. G; 9. A; 10. D.

GREED

Materials

- ❏ Construction paper
- ❏ Scissors
- ❏ Bible
- ❏ Gift wrap ribbon or paper strips (3/4 to 1 inch wide)
- ❏ Pencils and pens
- ❏ Glue sticks
- ❏ Ruler

Method

Just as the first commandment establishes the foundation for the other nine, the last commandment gives us insight into how we fail to observe some of the laws. "Coveting" is considered to be a source of sin. If we "have no other gods" and truly love our Creator with all our heart, soul, mind and strength, we will worship God and not harm or dishonor anything He has created. Similarly, if we really love our neighbor, we will not murder, commit adultery, steal or lie ... even in our thoughts! We will not covet anything that belongs to our neighbor.

"Covet" is a word we do not use very often in everyday conversation. A "covetous" person is greedy or has a strong desire for whatever belongs to someone else. Sometimes "covet" refers to being jealous or envious of another person's possessions or advantages. Coveting deals with thoughts rather than actions.

God's plan is that we spend more time thinking about His laws and less time worrying about what we have and do not have. Read Psalm 119:33-40. Verse 36 asks for God's help to "turn my heart to your decrees, and not to selfish gain."

Weave this small heart symbol to represent how all of the commandments are interwoven into two basic laws of love for God and our neighbor.

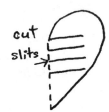

cut slits

Read the Ten Commandments (Exodus 20:1-17) and Psalm 119:33- 40. Choose a piece of colored paper and cut a 6 inch square. Fold the paper to cut a heart, using as much of the paper as possible. With the heart folded, cut three or four horizontal slits two inches long. Open the folded paper. The slits will be four inches long and almost as wide as the width of the heart.

Cut paper strips or ribbon into 12 inch lengths. Begin weaving by moving the "weaver" in and out or under and over the sections formed by the slits. Slide each band as close to the edge of the opening as possible. Fasten the strip at the top of the heart with the glue stick. Start the second weaver in an opposite section ... "over" if the first piece started "under" and so on ... alternating starting positions to form the woven pattern. There will be room for four or five ribbons or strips.

When the weaving is finished, be sure to secure the strips so they do not fall out. Along one of the curved edges at the top of the heart print, "Love God" and along the other curve, print "Love your neighbor." On the paper bands or ribbons that extend from the weaving beyond the bottom of the heart, write passages of scripture that show how the laws and teachings are interwoven. Choose from Exodus 20:1-17, especially Commandments 6,7,8,9 and 10; Psalm 119:33-40, and Mark 12:28-34. There will be room for a few key words from each passage. Add other scripture or your own ideas as a reminder that greed or jealousy can prevent us from loving God and our neighbor.

GOAL

Materials

- ❑ Paper
- ❑ Game sheets (one per participant)
- ❑ Duplicating equipment
- ❑ Pencils

Advance Preparation

☐ Duplicate a copy of the "_ _ _ _ _ _ _ _ _ _" GAME for each player.

Method

Exodus 20:17, the Tenth Commandment, reads "You shall not covet your neighbor's house; you shall not covet your neighbor's wife, or male or female slave, or ox, or donkey, or anything that belongs to your neighbor." (NRSV) If we were to rewrite the commandment in modern day language, we could add things like swimming pools, cars, motorcycles, designer clothes, home entertainment centers, video games, and so forth. One way to help understand, as well as to observe, the Tenth Commandment is to take the emphasis off of what we want, and to place it where it should be — on all the physical, emotional, and spiritual blessings that we have. If you were to start a list of your blessings, it would be very long and might include things ranging from health to happiness, computers to companions, and food to forgiveness.

Try playing a game that highlights just a few of God's blessings. Fill in each blank with the word described by the statement. The number of letters in the word are indicated by the number of spaces provided. Once you are finished, look at the first letter of each word and read them from top to bottom. You will discover a special statement about God's goodness to you! Write this sentence in the blanks on the top of the paper. It's the name of the game!

_ _ _ _ _ _ _ _ _ _ **GAME**

1. _ _ _ _ _ _ _ _   (Tasty treat that comes in many flavors)

2. _ _ _ _ _   (Red fruit that grows on trees)

3. _ _ _ _ _ _ _ _   (Prescriptions)

4. _ _ _ _ _   (Feathered, flying creatures)

5. _ _ _ _ _   (Mid-day meal)

6. _ _ _ _   (Organ used for sight)

7. _ _ _ _ _ _   (Building where students go to learn)

8. _ _ _ _ _ _ _   (Another name for house/home)

9. _ _ _ _ _ _   (Holiday to celebrate Jesus' resurrection)

10. _ _ _   (Canine pet)

ANSWERS

1. Ice Cream; 2. Apple; 3. Medicine; 4. Birds; 5. Lunch; 6. Eyes; 7.School; 8. Shelter; 9. Easter; 10. Dog. Title: I AM BLESSED.

GOSPEL

Method

- ❑ Heavy pellon interfacing
- ❑ Pencils
- ❑ Large file folders or cardstock
- ❑ Stapler and staples
- ❑ Bible
- ❑ Ruler
- ❑ Paper
- ❑ Scissors
- ❑ Envelopes
- ❑ Felt or flannel
- ❑ "F" encyclopedia
- ❑ Crayons

Method

There are many stories about people who have chosen to live according to God's word and the teachings of Jesus; and there are stories of individuals who have found God's way too difficult because of their covetous nature, greed, or selfishness. Two men for you to learn about are The Rich Ruler from Jesus' time and Saint Francis of Assisi, who lived in the Middle Ages.

The parable of The Rich Young Man is found in Matthew 19:16- 30, in Luke 18:18-30, and in Mark 10:17-31. The title may appear as The Rich Young Man, The Rich Man, or The Rich Ruler. It is reported that a wealthy young man asked Jesus what he must do to be a follower and to have eternal life. When Jesus answered that he must keep the commandments, the man replied that he had been faithful to the laws. Then Jesus explained one added requirement; he told the man to sell his possessions and to give the money to the poor. The man went away and was sad because he was asked to get rid of all of his belongings. Read the rest of the chapter to see what Jesus said to the disciples about rich people entering the kingdom of heaven.

Another rich young man, Francis, lived in the early 1200's in Assisi, Italy. He was captured while fighting in a local battle and was imprisoned for a few years. During his stay in prison, he saw much suffering and decided to change the way he lived. When he was set free, he gave up all of his wealth and lived a life of poverty ... just the opposite of coveting! He devoted his life to building churches and helping the poor. Francis served as a missionary and was declared a saint in 1228, after his death. Saint Francis of Assisi was known for his love of nature and all living things, as well as for his life of service. He shared many religious beliefs in his writings and poetry. Discover more about this interesting man by checking biographical resources.

Depict one of these stories in the form of a flannelgraph and retell it to others by using your original visual aids! Decide what figures and scenery you will need to tell the story. On scrap paper, draw people and objects in proportion to the folder provided. You may be able to trace pictures from resource materials. Place the interfacing over the drawings or book illustrations and trace. Color the tracings with crayons and cut out. When all of the pieces are finished, place in an envelope and set aside.

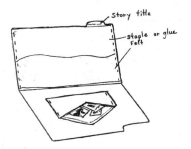

Measure and cut the flannel or felt to fit the folder. Staple the fabric to the tab side of the folder. On the other part of the folder, staple the envelope flap in open position. This will allow you to keep your story pieces with the background. Label the tab or top edge of the folder with the story title. Tell the story by placing the pieces on the background material. The interfacing will adhere to the fabric. Prepare to share your story with a friend or family member.

GENEROSITY

Materials

- ❏ Copies of poems
- ❏ Gift wrap
- ❏ Tape
- ❏ Pens
- ❏ Small boxes
- ❏ Ribbon
- ❏ Scissors
- ❏ Glue

Advance Preparation

- ❏ Make photocopies of the following poem:

> This is a very special gift
>
> That you can never see
>
> The reason it's so special is
>
> It's just for you from me.
>
>
> Whenever you are lonely
>
> Or maybe feeling blue
>
> You only have to hold this gift
>
> And know I think of you.
>
>
> You never should unwrap it
>
> Just leave the ribbon tied
>
> And hold the box close to your heart
>
> It's filled with love inside.

Method

It is not unusual to want something which someone else has. We all like to own nice things! There is nothing wrong with working hard to earn a new bicycle, buying a new outfit for a special occasion, or receiving a "wished for" gift. The Tenth Commandment guides us to avoid setting our hearts on something that is not ours and to keep from resenting what others have.

God wants us to be happy with what we have and to accept gratefully the "gifts" we have been given. Everyone has unique talents, abilities and characteristics that make us who we are. There will always be individuals who are prettier, smarter, richer and more popular than we are; at the same time, there will always be people who have much less than we have.

Think of the opposite of "coveting." It might be "giving" or "generosity." Instead of wasting our time and energy resenting others, it seems God would like to see us use what we already have. You can help someone in a school subject that is easy for you; you can run an errand or help with simple chores for a busy mom or a person with a walker; or you can save some of your allowance or earned money for a donation to a charity. You are not too young to practice good stewardship ... sharing your time, talent and money. One of the most generous gifts you can give is yourself and another precious gift is your love. You can lend a helping hand, you can listen or just be there!

This project is a reminder for your friends and loved ones that you are trying to be a "giver" not someone who "covets." Select a small box and cover it with gift wrap and tie with ribbon. Attach a copy of the poem to the top of the box. Give the box to someone as a symbol of the generous gift of yourself and of your love.

Summary Of The Law

In Matthew 22:37-40 Jesus summarizes the ten negative "You Shall Nots" of Exodus 20:1-17 and Deuteronomy 5:1-22 into two positive "You Shalls." When the lawyer tried to test Jesus with the question "Which commandment in the law is the greatest," Jesus referred to two Old Testament Scripture passages for his answer. "You shall love the Lord your God with all your heart, and with all your soul, and with all your mind" is a direct quotation of Deuteronomy 6:5, and the words "You shall love your neighbor as yourself" are recorded in Leviticus 19:18.

The verse which Jesus quotes in Deuteronomy 6:5 is part of the Shema, the basic and essential creed of Judaism. It means that we must give God a total love—a love which dominates our emotions, a love which directs our thoughts, and a love which is the dynamic of our actions. This love is expressed through a total commitment of life to God.

Referring to the words of Leviticus 19:18 Jesus reminded the lawyer, as well as all of us, that our love for God must issue forth in love for others. And, others are loveable because they are made in the image of God (Genesis 1:26, 27)

In Jesus' summary of the law he does not abolish the Ten Commandments, rather he enriches them and puts them into a perspective that is easy for us to remember and to follow. In order to gain a better understanding of the Summary of the Law, and its application for life today, use the five learning activities provided in this chapter. Each experience focuses on a phrase of Matthew 22:37-40. "Love" — heart, "Letter" — soul, "Language" — mind, "Lesson" — neighbor, and "Likeness" — self, all offer ways to explore God's Old Testament teaching and Jesus' New Testament interpretation and to make them real and relevant for living a life of love today.

LOVE

Materials

- Black construction paper
- Colored tissue paper
- Waxed paper
- Glue brushes
- Bible
- Scrap paper
- Heart pattern
- Black permanent markers
- Scissors
- Containers for glue
- Pencils
- Tape

Method

In the first five books of the Old Testament, the Torah, there were 613 laws given to the Hebrew people. Christians consider the Ten Commandments to be the most essential of all laws and regard them as guidelines for "right living."

Jesus made it a lot easier for us to remember the laws by summarizing them into two parts: love for God and love for our neighbor. If we obey these two laws, we will be following all of the Ten Commandments! Can you explain how?

Read the Scripture passage in Matthew 22:37-40. Jesus tells us that loving God is the most important law to remember. We are instructed to love God with all of our heart, soul and mind.

If we love God with all of our heart, we are loving and worshiping with all of our human emotions. We usually think of praising God in terms of joyful or happy feelings. How can you honor God with other emotions? You can be angry because of human injustice or sad because of destruction of God's creation—and do something about it!

Another way to "love God with all of your heart" is to promise to love Him and to obey His laws. When we make the promise or commitment to love and to live according to God's laws, it is said that "The laws are written in our hearts."

David, the Psalm writer, expresses heartfelt love for God in many songs and prayers. In Psalm 40:8 he says: "I desire to do your will, O my God; your law is within my heart." In Psalm 86:12, which is a prayer, David says, "I will praise you, O Lord my God, with all my heart: I will glorify your name forever."

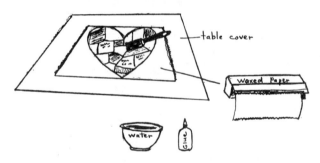

Make a "see-through" heart collage with "feeling" words that show how you can love God. You may want to add verses from the Psalms or other scripture.

Read the passages from Psalm 40:8 and Psalm 86:12, as well as Matthew 22:37-40. Make a list of emotions or of feeling words that could be used to demonstrate devotion to God.

Brush thinned glue onto the waxed paper surface and arrange tissue pieces all over the glued area. With permanent marker, write the words or scripture you have chosen—scattering them around the heart.

For a glossy look, brush glue over the surface of tissue and writing. Set the tissue-covered waxed paper aside to dry. Place the heart pattern over black paper, trace and cut out a "frame." Tape or glue the heart-shaped frame over the collage. Make sure the heart opening is large enough for most of the tissue area and all of the writing to be in view.

Tape the finished collage to a window allowing light to shine through. Learn the lines of scripture "by heart" to demonstrate your love for God.

LETTER

Materials

- Bible
- Pencils and pens
- Stamps
- Paper
- Envelopes

Method

Throughout the Bible, the term "heart and soul" is used to explain our relationship to our Creator. Look up Deuteronomy 4:29, Deuteronomy 30:2, and Matthew 22:37-40. In the Matthew verses we are instructed to love God with our whole heart, soul and mind.

If we define "heart" as emotion or feeling, then we may think of "soul" as the very essence of a human being. The soul is the center of a person's energy and individuality—it is "who you are!"

The Ten Commandments given to Moses were written on stone; those tablets have been lost for thousands of years. Throughout history, the laws have been written down in many forms. We know that books and writings can be destroyed, but the laws themselves will not disappear. Similarly, the human body dies and disappears, but the soul is the part of who you are that never dies.

To show how much you love God, your energy and actions must be centered on following His plan. Your whole being, or in other words, your whole life must be committed to God.

Re-read the Ten Commandments (Deuteronomy 5:1-22) and think about how those laws that were written so long ago can apply to you today. Make a list of ways you can change your actions or the way you live: I will try hard to be honest and to tell the truth always; "I will not talk back to my parents;" "I will not use bad language."

In this activity, write a letter to yourself listing three changes you will try to make in your life. Write a short letter explaining what you would like to change and why. Pray for God to help you keep your promises. Carefully address the letter to yourself and seal the envelope. Arrange for the teacher or another adult to mail the letter to you in two or three months.

When you receive the letter, see if you have been able to keep the promises you made. Remember that no matter how hard we try to become a better person, we will continue to make mistakes. Whatever our blunder, God will forgive us if we are sorry and if we ask for His help.

LANGUAGE

Materials

- Pencils
- Green tissue paper
- Scissors
- Bamboo skewers or thin dowels
- Flower pots or paper cups, small
- Red and pink construction paper
- Green floral tape
- Clay
- Glue
- Dictionary

Method

In Jesus' summary of the Ten Commandments, he instructs us to love God with all of our mind. Look up the word "mind" in a dictionary. It is a hard term to define. Basically, it means "thoughts." Think about ways to love God with your thoughts. Sometimes thoughts are spoken, however, many times they go unsaid. All of our thoughts related to God, to others, and to ourselves should center on the theme of love. There are many ways to express love. Make a flower in the form of the sign language symbol for "I Love You" as a reminder of this part of the Summary of the Law.

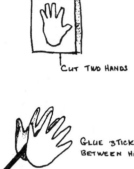

CUT TWO HANDS

GLUE STICK BETWEEN HANDS

Stack red and pink construction paper and trace your hand with thumb extended onto the sheets. Cut both hands at once so they are the same size or cut out one hand using it as a pattern for the contrasting paper.

Twist floral tape around the stick and attach leaves or tufts of tissue paper to complete the stem. Glue construction paper hands together, enclosing the top portion of the stem. Fold down the middle and ring fingers, then glue them to the palm.

Press a lump of clay into the bottom of a paper cup or small flowerpot. Secure the stem and "flower" by pressing them firmly into the center of the clay. Be certain the plant is balanced and is upright. Surround the stem with crumpled, colored tissue to hide the clay.

Share this expression of your thoughts with a friend or place it in a location that will remind you of your love for God and for others.

LESSON

Materials

- ❑ Paper
- ❑ Markers
- ❑ Scissors
- ❑ Bible

Method

"Love your neighbor as yourself" is a big order to fill. One way to keep this law is to look at Jesus' other instructions concerning love. In addition to the summary of the Ten Commandments recorded in Matthew 22:37-40, our Master Teacher gave good advice in Matthew 7:12. Often called the Golden Rule, "In everything do to others as you would have them do to you," we are told to give the love we would like to get in return — a good guideline for loving our neighbor as ourself.

cut away corners

Offer a tangible expression of love to someone by making and giving a unique card-coupon. Cut paper, about 5 1/2" x 8 1/2". Fold in half crosswise. Cut a 1 1/2" x 2 1/2" piece from the top right-hand corner. Fold down along the dotted line, then snip this part into a heart shape. Push the heart so that it's folded inside the card. Write on the card an intended activity or service such as weeding the garden, raking the leaves, or sharing a picnic or game. When the card is opened, the heart will pop up.

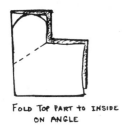
FOLD TOP PART to INSIDE ON ANGLE

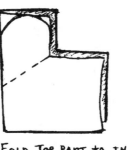

FOLD TOP PART to INSIDE ON ANGLE

LIKENESS

Materials

- ❑ Small mirrors
- ❑ Shells, beads, buttons, ribbon or fabric trims
- ❑ Tacky glue or glue gun
- ❑ Self-stick labels

Method

When Jesus summarized the Ten Commandments into two laws of love, he instructed his followers to love God with heart, soul and mind; and then he said: "You shall love your neighbor as yourself." It has been said that you really cannot love someone else unless you have love and respect for yourself.

Does it seem strange that you should love yourself? Having respect for yourself is not the same thing as being self-centered or conceited. Remember that you were chosen to be born as a special part of God's creation. We are all made with some of the same characteristics of God; that is, made in the image of God. Have you ever heard the saying, "God doesn't make junk"?

When we feel worthy of God's love and feel that we are entitled to love from the people around us, it is easier to love our neighbor.

Think about all of the special traits you have instead of any shortcomings. Maybe you do not have the best grades, but you are a fast runner; maybe your hair never seems to look right to you, but you are a loyal friend. Make a list of the things that you think are unique about YOU. How can you show love for a neighbor by sharing one of your special gifts?

Decorate a small mirror as a reminder that you are made in God's image and that you are worthy of receiving and giving love.

Wash and dry the mirror. Choose the items you like from the selection of supplies and make a border to decorate the mirror's frame. Apply glue, a little at a time, then stick on decorations in a pleasing arrangement. Allow the glue to dry thoroughly.

You might want to attach a small label to the back of your mirror with a reminder for you: [Name], made in the image of God, or maybe a list of words to help you feel worthy of being loved.

Ten Commandment Review

Directions. Guideposts. Instructions. Precepts. Maps. Patterns. Signs. All of these words, plus many others, describe the Ten Commandments. Lewis Smedes in his book Mere Morality [Grand Rapids, MI: Eerdmans, 1983] also calls them "designs" and "invitations." "[God] who pointed us to His design for living at Mount Sinai embraces us with His love at Mount Calvary. He who pins us down with demands at every nook and cranny of life frees us from any and all condemnation. Once forgiven, we hear His commands, not as a burden, but as an invitation to enjoy our humanity, and in our joy to glorify our Creator."

Use the activities in this chapter, the last in the series on the Ten Commandments, as a way to help participants relate God's "Laws to Love By" to their lives. Categorizing these guidelines, recorded in Exodus 20:1-17 and Deuteronomy 5:1-22, as Directions, Instructions, Patterns, Rules and Signs, will help students learn to apply and appreciate the Commandments as the basis for their relationship with God and with others.

DIRECTIONS

Materials

- ❑ Bible
- ❑ Pencils
- ❑ Construction paper
- ❑ Glue sticks
- ❑ Ruler
- ❑ Bulletin board space or poster board
- ❑ Letter patterns
- ❑ Scissors
- ❑ Stapler and staples
- ❑ Markers
- ❑ Gold foil paper

Method

The Ten Commandments are precepts that "point the way" or the direction for each of us. When we give someone directions, we describe a route or a course of action. Another way we can give directions is to explain procedures for completing a task. The commandments provide standards which govern our relationship to God and to each other. God directs us in the way to live morally in our religious and civil dealings. When we learn the Ten Commandments and observe them each day, we are following God's plan.

Design a bulletin board or poster that inspires viewers to consider God's directions as summarized in the Ten Commandments.

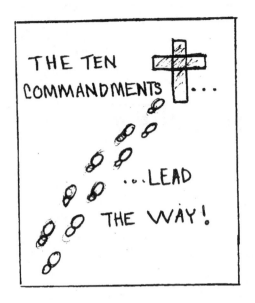

Locate the Ten Commandments in your Bible (Exodus 20:1-17 and Deuteronomy 5:1-22) and place a bookmark to save the place. Gather the materials needed to assemble a bulletin board or poster. Use dark-colored background ... either posterboard or covering for the bulletin board surface.

Trace and cut letters to spell out the caption: "The Ten Commandments Lead the Way." Select a color that contrasts with the background. Another method for lettering is to use a wide-tipped marker to print the letters. Place the caption on the upper third of the backing material.

Make a pattern for a foot step. Trace around your shoe if you are working on a large display area; draw a mini-foot shape for a small bulletin board or a poster. Trace and cut ten foot-steps from colors of construction paper which contrast with the background. Rainbow colors would make an attractive arrangement. Copy the Ten Commandments from the Bible ... one on each footstep. Cut a large cross from the gold foil.

Arrange the shapes either of the following ways. The foot-steps may lead to the centered gold cross or the cross may be placed off to one side with the steps leading to it. Experiment with the placement. When you like the way it looks, glue or staple the pieces in place.

Display your design for others to see. Consider making this project in a very small form to be used as a postcard or notepaper for friendly correspondence or thank you notes!

INSTRUCTIONS

Materials

- ❏ Bibles
- ❏ Pencils or pens
- ❏ Index cards
- ❏ Paper
- ❏ Markers
- ❏ Other supplies will vary with selected activities

Method

God has provided for us a concise "how-to-do-it" manual for "right living." His special "how-to" instructions are known as The Ten Commandments. When we are learning the correct way to do something, we follow instructions very carefully. In some instances we know the steps "by heart" ... we have them memorized.

The laws God has given us to follow are so important that we should memorize them! In Psalm 119:9-11, we are reminded of the value of God's law:

''How can young people keep their way pure?

By guarding it according to Your word.

With my whole heart I seek You;

Do not let me stray from Your commandments.

I treasure Your word in my heart, so that I may not

sin against You."

Do you have a particular method you use to memorize school lessons? Learn the commandments "by heart" using a process that works for you or experiment with one of the methods explained in this activity. Most of these methods can be used to review by yourself, but many would be fun to do with a friend, as well.

Read the Ten Commandments several times (Exodus 20: 1-17 or Deuteronomy 5:1-22). Then use one, a few, or ALL ten of the following methods to help you memorize the list of commandments!

1. **CLOTHESLINE.** Print each commandment on a separate sheet of paper, then clip them in order onto a cord or small clothesline. Close your eyes, remove a paper and place it face down. Read the list to determine which law is missing. Continue until the clothesline is empty.

2. **SCRAMBLED COMMANDMENTS.** Write each commandment on a note card. Prepare all ten cards by gluing on a magnetic strip or a piece of sandpaper. Place the cards face down and scramble them. Turn the cards over and see if you can put them in order. Arrange the cards with magnets on the side of a file cabinet or refrigerator. Use a flannel board to display the cards with sandpaper strips.

3. **FLASHCARDS.** Number cards from one to ten with Roman numerals. On the opposite side of each card, print the correct commandment. Stack the cards in order by number, then test yourself to see if you know what is on the other side. Try it both ways: Read the numbers, then give the correct commandment or view the words and decide which number relates.

4. **CONCENTRATION.** Write out two sets of cards for each of the ten laws. Mix up the cards and place them face down in rows on the table. Turn over two cards. If they are a match, set the cards aside; if not, flip them over and continue turning over pairs until all of the cards are matched.

5. **TAPE RECORDING.** Record yourself reading the Ten Commandments. Listen to the tape and at various intervals, push the pause button to see if you can finish the list. Listen to the tape over and over for review.

6. **REPETITION.** Locate the commandments in the Bible and read the list several times. Cover the words, then try to recite as much of the passage as possible. Continue to re-read, cover up and recite until the verses are memorized.

7. **PARAPHRASE.** Read the Ten Commandments in the Bible. Think about the meaning of each one, then try to paraphrase or explain in your own words. Fold a piece of paper in half, lengthwise. On one side of the fold, copy the list of God's laws; on the other side of the paper, write the laws in your own words.

8. **KEY WORDS.** Carefully read the Ten Commandments. Pick out one or a few key words that clearly represent each commandment. Test yourself to see if you can recall the complete verse with the key word reminder.

9. **MEMORY CHAIN.** Cut construction paper into ten strips. Print one commandment, with its number included, on each strip. Practice reading and

reviewing the "rules" until you remember them. As you memorize a commandment, add that link to the chain. They may be out of order on the chain, but you will have learned the correct number as part of the entire commandment.

10. **VISUAL REMINDER.** Create a small banner or sign in the shape of the tablets of stone. Print or type "The Ten Commandments" and add a decorative border. Display the banner where you will see it many times during the day, such as on your mirror, desk, notebook or locker. Seeing the list will help you to memorize the laws.

Memorizing the Ten Commandments or any other scripture passage is very important for people who want to live following God's instructions. However, to "treasure" God's word in your heart includes understanding the meaning and living accordingly, as well as memorizing the words!

PATTERN

Materials

- ❑ Lightweight cardboard
- ❑ Pencils
- ❑ Toothpicks
- ❑ Dental floss or colored string
- ❑ Miscellaneous beads

- ❑ Ruler
- ❑ Scissors
- ❑ Glue and glue brushes or glue sticks
- ❑ Beading needle
- ❑ Magazines or colorful bulletin covers

Method

The Ten Commandments are considered to be a very special pattern for living. God summarized the covenant-agreement with His people and provided a "How-to-do-it" pattern for living when the laws were handed down to Moses. The Ten Commandments provide us with a pattern for how to worship our Creator and how to behave toward other people. Patterns are designs or models that serve as good examples for making something or doing something.

There are all types of patterns made for anything that is built or constructed. An architect draws blueprints for a building design. What do you think would happen if the builder did not follow the plans exactly? What would happen if clothing was sewn without the help of a properly measured pattern? When you create artwork, assemble models or make crafts and toys, you need some kind of example or pattern. It is important to follow plans in order to have a good end result.

Follow the simple pattern for these paper beads and create a friendship bracelet or necklace. Carefully make a pattern that will help you form each bead. On the cardboard, measure a one-inch by 9-inch triangle. Cut out the long, narrow shape and trace ten times on a magazine page or bulletin cover. Cut the triangular strips apart. Brush a small amount of glue along the length of the strip, lay a toothpick across the wide end of the paper and roll the paper tightly to the point. Continue until all of the beads are finished.

Make ten beads, one for each commandment and for added interest, alternate with plastic or glass beads. Measure enough string for a bracelet or necklace. String the beads and tie to secure. Use a beading needle, if the bead holes are small.

cut apart triangles

roll up paper strip

If you follow the pattern and example carefully, you will have an attractive reminder of the Ten Commandments ... our pattern for living.

RULES

Materials

- ❏ Materials to form hopscotch game—chalk, masking tape, carpet squares
- ❏ Bible
- ❏ Beanbags or stones

Advance Preparation

- ❏ Make a hopscotch game to use for the activity. If the game can be played outside, draw a traditional hopscotch game in the dirt or in chalk on the sidewalk. If it is to be played indoors, lay one out with carpet squares. Use masking tape to make a number on each square. If carpet squares aren't available, use masking tape to make both squares and numbers.

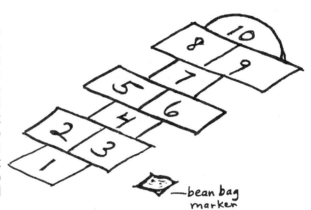

—bean bag marker

Method

Every game has rules—the established procedures for playing the activity. Sometimes the Ten Commandments are called "Rules" too. In order to be used as rules for living we must do more than just learn the laws—we must understand what they mean for every day situations. Play a game of "Commandment Hopscotch." Follow the rules and use the activity as an opportunity to relate the commandments to your own life.

Use the hopscotch game provided, outside or indoors, and select a marker such as a stone or beanbag. Throw the marker into one of the numbered squares. Remember to hop on one foot in the single squares, land on both feet in the double squares, and hop over the square that holds the marker. When you land on a block, summarize the commandment that goes with the number in the square. On each turn recite one of the commandments in your own words! For example, 8—I will be honest on a test, or 10—I will not blame my brother for something that I did. Play the game until you have hopped to the top of the "board" and back to the beginning.

SIGNS

Materials

- ❏ Chenille stems (extra long pipe cleaners)
- ❏ Scissors
- ❏ Tissue paper, cellophane, mylar, foil or construction paper
- ❏ Shallow containers such as margarine tubs

- ❏ Plaster of Paris
- ❏ Pencils
- ❏ Glue
- ❏ Cardboard
- ❏ Water
- ❏ Newspaper (for covering work surfaces)

- ❏ "Sign" pictures and patterns
- ❏ Tape
- ❏ Stapler and staples
- ❏ Container or bucket for mixing plaster
- ❏ Polyfill or roll of cotton

Method

Think of all of the different traffic signs you see every day. Stop. Go. Merge. Yield. One Way. On a sheet of paper, write down as many signs as possible. Each of these markers, plus many others, could be matched with one of the Ten Commandments as another way to help understand God's laws.

Number a sheet of paper from one to ten. Try writing the commandment next to each number. Look at the list of signs again and try to pair one sign with each commandment. Although some signs, like "Stop" and Go," might be used to illustrate several of God's laws, limit the choice to the most meaningful symbol for each Commandment. Here are some suggestions:

One Way
Commandment One - "You shall have no other gods before me"

No Parking
Commandment Two - "You shall not make for yourself an idol ..."

Go
Commandment Four - "Remember the sabbath day, and keep it holy."

Stop
Commandment Six - "You shall not kill"

School Crossing
Commandment Eight - "You shall not steal"

International No Sign
Commandment Ten - "You shall not covet"

Using these ideas, create a type of sculpture called a stabile. Explain that a stabile has small parts like a mobile, but instead of hanging or swinging freely, the parts are fastened into a base. For this project ten "road" signs, each representing a different commandment, will be used in the sculpture.

Select ten pipe cleaners, different types of paper, as well as pencils and scissors. Glue, tape, or staplers are also needed for the project. Trace and cut two of the same "signs" for each pipe cleaner. "Sandwich" the pipe cleaner between two same-sized paper symbols. Fasten with glue, tape or staples. For a more sculptural look, poke a small bit of cotton or polyfill into some of the larger signs just before fastening. Continue until all "Signs" are attached to the pipe cleaners. Set aside.

Work with a leader to mix plaster of paris for the base of the stabile. Carefully follow the directions on the plaster package! When the mixture is the right consistency, pour slowly into the shallow containers. When the plaster begins to set up, the surface will feel warm. Insert each pipe cleaner securely into the plaster. Arrange the "Signs" so there are various sizes, colors, textures, and stem lengths. Hands must be washed thoroughly when finished with the base. Allow the plaster to harden. The base will look more attractive if covered with paper, such as tissue paper.

Set the stabile in a place where the "Signs" will serve as reminders of God's laws for living a life of love.

CHAPTER FOURTEEN

Enhancements

Although the information and ideas contained in the book <u>Laws To Love By: The Ten Commandments</u> are presented in a Learning Center format, the contents and concepts can be easily adapted for use in various worship, education, outreach, and nurture settings within a congregation. Try the suggestions for "ten" areas of ministry and add others to modify the material and methods to meet specific situations and circumstances.

Adult Bible Study

- Research and report on the customs and culture of the time in which God gave the Ten Commandments.

- Study a "Commandment of the Month" and include Biblical, historical, and modern day interpretations of it.

Children's Church/Worship

- Create a children's bulletin using many of the "paper and pencil" activities from the Learning Centers.

- Incorporate information about each Commandment into a series of children's messages.

Confirmation Classes

- Interview members of the congregation, such as Pastors and Church School teachers, who have put the Commandments into practice in their own lives.

- Show videos highlighting the themes of the Commandments.

Intergenerational Events

- Depict the essence of each Commandment in a "Living Tableau," a representation of a scene by an individual or a group dressed in costume.

- Highlight information about each Commandment in a "This Is Your Life" format.

Outreach

- Become involved in a local, regional, national or international project that emphasizes God's "laws to love by."

- Emphasize ways of showing love to the hungry, thirsty, stranger, poor, sick, and imprisoned.

Sunday School

- Make a mural or a bulletin board picturing the theme of each Commandment.

- Present a program, such as a puppet show, illustrating ways in which the Commandments are put into practice.

Vacation Bible School

- Design a Vacation Bible School program on the theme of the Ten Commandments.

- Integrate the Learning Center activities into a Bible times setting.

Week Day Programs - After School Care; Kid's Clubs

- Organize an Art Exhibit of items created in the learning centers.

- Teach hymns and hymn stories on the theme of each Commandment.

Worship

- Display banners related to each Commandment.

- Preach a sermon series on the themes of the Commandments.

Youth Groups

- Initiate a service project, short-term or long-term, to demonstrate the theme of one or more of the Commandments.

- Produce a video on "The Ten Commandments" in action.

Resources

Blanch, Stuart. The Ten Commandments. Atlanta, GA: Episcopal Radio-TV Foundation, 1981.

Davidman, Joy. Smoke On The Mountain - An Interpretation Of The Ten Commandments. Philadelphia: Westminster, 1954.

Drew, George E. The Ten Commandments In Today's World. Prescott, AZ: Educational Ministries, Inc., 1979.

Editors. The Children's Bible - The Old Testament - The New Testament. New York: Golden Press, 1965.

Editors. Great Stories From The Old Testament. Waco, TX: Creative Resources, 1976.

Halley, Henry H. Halley's Bible Handbook. Chicago, IL: Henry H. Halley, 1st edition 1924, 21st edition revised, 1957.

McBride, Alfred. The Ten Commandments. Sounds Of Love From Sinai. Cincinnati, OH: St. Anthony Messenger Press, 1990.

Murphy, William, Editor. The Ten Commandments For Children. New York: The Regina Press, 1980.

Schaeffer, Edith. Lifelines. The Ten Commandments For Today. Westchester, IL: Crossway Books, 1982.

Smedes, Lewis B. Mere Morality: What God Expects From Ordinary People. Grand Rapids, MI: Eerdmans, 1983.

Truitt, Gloria A. The Ten Commandments. Learning About God's Law. St Louis, MO: Concordia, 1983.